DEATH OBJECT

Death Object

Exploding the Nuclear Weapons Hoax

Akio Nakatani

Copyright © 2017 Akio Nakatani

The moral right of the author has been asserted.

All rights reserved.
No part of this publication may be reproduced, stored in a retrieval system, or transmitted, in any form or by any means, without the prior permission in writing of the publisher, nor be otherwise circulated in any form of binding or cover other than that in which it is published and without a similar condition including this condition being imposed on the subsequent purchaser.

Print ISBN 978-1-5455-1683-6

CONTENTS

Prologue	1
Introduction: SATAN 2	3
Fire Last Time	8
Fire This Time	16
Born Secret	18
Enemy At the Gates	18
Geek-Out	21
Pinball as Extinction Level Event	22
Binding Energy	24
Stonewall	28
The Nuclear Secret That Dare Not Speak Its Name	31
Burn the Sky!	32
Virtual Manhattan Project	33
Checkmate	48
The Secret	61
Money Shot: TRINITY	71
Something Like an Actor	72
Unit Testing?	74
Jumbo	77
100-Ton Test	80
I Am Become Death	88
Trinitite	94

Fool Me Twice: Japan 1945   **96**
   Hiroshima   96
      Little Boy   97
      Firestorm!   103
      Seversky   114
      What's Going On?   118
      Medical Testimony   132
      Fire in the Hole!   135
      Matsushige Photographs   148
      No Bald Spot   153
   Trickery is the Way of War   158
   Nagasaki   170
   Downfall   178

The Mike of the Beast   **183**
   H-Bomb   183
   Lookout Mountain Studios   186
   Something Fishy: Bikini   189
   Photo and Film Checklist   198

Conspiracy!   **201**

Fire No Time: Falsification   **209**

Acknowledgements   **211**

Bibliography   **212**

About the Author   **217**

Prologue

兵者詭道也
Trickery is the way of war.

Sunzi

The process of atomic fission produces all kinds of elemental "stuff":

> *Plutonium and uranium split unevenly. It is rare that they split into two equal parts, and in the explosion their fragments become every element below them. Anything you can name is there – molybdenum, barium, iodine, cesium, strontium, antimony, hydrogen, tin, copper, carbon, iron, silver, and gold.*

('The Curve of Binding Energy' John McPhee)

In that eclectic spirit, this book can be read as a critical assembly of many different elemental traces: primer (*Nuclear Bombs for Dummies*), history, polemic, prophecy, comedy or tragedy. If you think this topic's gray and gloomy gravitas rules out any of those, watch Stanley Kubrick's masterpiece of atomic humor, *Dr. Stranglove*, and think again.

If you're already an atomic skeptic, this book will serve as a handy reference compendium of familiar evidence coherently organized. If you're a firm believer in the reality of nuclear weapons, this book could make you think twice. If you haven't considered the subject one way or the other, I can promise you that by the end of this book you'll have received a larger dosage of nuclear knowledge with less strain and boredom than you'd have thought humanly possible. If I get you thinking more seriously about the implications of atomic weaponry, then as far as I'm concerned – *result*!

Keep one thing in mind as you read. In addition to all the junky byproducts of a nuclear blast listed above, there's one other: *photon emissions*. That's visible light and it's what I hope this book can radiate. I think you'll find it both enlightening (like a stimulating course lecture) and entertaining (like a horror movie).

How could a topic so unthinkably ghastly be *entertaining*? I don't mean to disrespect the suffering of anybody injured or killed in any war, by any means – conventional or otherwise. In this world of madness and pain, we need gallows humor. I use levity to reduce our risk of ending up like noted historian Iris Chang, who (it is speculated), spiraled into suicidal depression after interviewing one too many of the survivors of the 20th century's worst horrors.

As a counter-balance, I advise all readers to browse the Hiroshima memoir *Barefoot Gen* (manga by Keiji Nakazawa) in parallel. Whenever you tire of the occasional witticism or moment of sarcastic levity in this book, revert to *Barefoot Gen*. Absorb the madness and mainline the stupefying graphic atrocity as a mood-corrective. The conventional understanding of nuclear history is as true in its function of allegory and metaphor (or warning and prophecy) as it is false in its literal facts.

Introduction: SATAN 2

God gave Noah the rainbow sign,
No more water, the fire next time.

Traditional

In May of 2016, Russian state news outlet Sputnik reported on the latest incarnation of the devil that has dogged humanity these seventy-plus years: the RS-28 Sarmat intercontinental ballistic missile, which can carry a variable number of warheads. According to Wikipedia, at maximum throw-weight of 10,000 kilograms, this doomsday machine can deliver a 50 megaton charge. It's a shotgun version of the largest single explosive device ever deployed, the 'Tsar Bomba', supposedly tested by the Soviets, weighing in around 55 megatons yield – more than all the ordnance used in World War II (including the atomic bombs) combined. The RS-28 Sarmat ('Satan 2') can wipe out Texas or France.

Or can it? Hmmm. Only one way to find out: *3... 2... 1 – hit that red button*: 'FIRE IN THE HOLE!'

If the above weapon exists, it (and its brothers) *will* be used - sooner more likely than later. Psychopaths run the world. The classic movie *Dr. Strangelove* will easily convince you that all a nation's top cabal needs is some confidence that their central mil.gov officials (and a few buddies and lovers) have at least a roach's chance to survive the enemy's counterpunch, and they will *bring it*. As for non-state actors, they may not care about self-preservation, in which case none of the elaborately gamed deterrence theory (Mutual Assured Destruction, the Prisoner's Dilemma, the Nash Equilibrium, and the like) is worth spit.

But hang on a sec – is *fire in the hole* truly the only way to determine the credibility of the Satan 2 or any nuclear weapon? Is there no rational resting place between fear-porn foreplay and the money shot that ends the world? There *is* a calm eye in this storm - the fact that nuclear weapons don't work, don't exist. This book explores the claim that *nuclear weapons do not function, they are a large-scale hoax.* I call this hoax the Fake Nuke Feint.

> **feint**: noun
>
> 1. *a deceptive or pretended blow, thrust, or other movement, especially in boxing or fencing.* "a brief feint at the opponent's face"

Who exactly 'the opponent' might be remains as a research topic. I'm just going to lay out the relevant technical and social considerations without pointing fingers at specific individuals or particular institutions.

Why this book:

- To *assemble* relevant arguments and evidence
- To *organize* arguments and evidence for easy access and navigation
- To *filter out* irrelevant points, ill-logic, ill-will and prejudice
- To *disseminate* key questions for wider awareness
- To *stimulate* further discussion and research

A treatment of a hot topic like the fundamental feasibility of nuclear weapons needs some justification, framing and scene-setting. The immediate expected reaction, from a sane, rational, and educated audience, is the *ad hominem* kill-shot below:

> *This author is just another internet conspiracy nut.*

I won't blame you for that knee jerk. After all, this book lays out a wild proposition. It's also an inconvenient truth, because *I cannot reveal the technical clincher*. I'm forced to circle the issue, and use a megaton of circumstantial evidence to do the clearance that a single gram of the direct, incontrovertible but un-publishable counter-science would accomplish. Since that result cannot be openly published, this book boils down partly to a review of *circumstantial* challenges to the nuclear weapons orthodoxy. Though I could nuke the entire orthodoxy with the scientific result (*beyond a reasonable doubt*), unfortunately due to archaic USA national security laws I can only carpet-bomb the topic with circumstantial material and inference (*preponderance of the evidence*).

The material is a mix of 'new stuff', sourced from me, blended with existing historical and technical evidence scattered across the web, books and films. Even if you work with highest beyond-top-secret clearance at a nuclear weapons design facility, don't feel superior to those in the Outer Darkness. We're all in the same boat. Amateur nuke debunkers, concerned analysts like me, academic scientists of every stripe, and yes, you too, whoever you are – when it comes to nukes, we're *all* just rats beneath the mil.gov's high table. For the foreseeable future (because of the security laws), we can only gnaw at whatever scraps have slopped down to the public domain. Yet by means of those scraps I have discovered 'the nuclear secret that dare not speak its name'.

This book is based entirely on unclassified public materials. As you can see from the Bibliography, those mostly consist of mainstream histories and technical manuals, compiled by qualified and knowledgeable authorities. It's overwhelmingly respectable, intellectual, clinical, responsible stuff. Additionally, over the past few years a small community of internet nuclear skeptics has developed. They occasionally display a spark of useful comment or the glowing ember of a little-known citation. We may enjoy dissing them as paranoid nutcases, but I feel that, if nothing else, we should admire their guts in holding to a contrarian stance in this world of fearful conformity. Unfortunately, their stuff suffers from contamination with both *prejudice* and *distraction*.

The prejudices are the usual tsunami of keyboard hate, directed at one or another ethnic or religious group(s) suspected of secretly pulling the strings. I have no idea how that disgusting and reprehensible ethnic hatred has crept into, or perhaps originally motivated, investigation of nuclear weapons. Read my lips: *this book has zero connection with any ideology or propaganda of hate*.

Prejudice and hate are the symptoms of a vile mental illness, for which I have no tolerance whatsoever. Hate speech is also irrelevant to the technical, cultural and political topic at hand, which is one thing and one thing alone: *the feasibility of explosive nuclear weapons.*

Even when existing skeptical materials are bias-free, they often suffer from muddled focus. Conspiracy people, by the nature of their game, want to connect all dots and enlarge the picture as much as possible. Thus, on any given site devoted to exploring the nuclear weapons hoax, you'll usually find interleaved discussion of other presumed hoaxes, with links to scams and (putative) 'false flag' operations, such as the JFK assassination, the Apollo moon landings, the Oklahoma City bombing, and 9-11 as an inside job. This book takes no position on any of those attractive nuisances. For this book, I don't care about any of that. This book is rigidly circumscribed to one thing and one thing alone: the *Fake Nuke Feint.*

The core of this analysis is my own research result. Since I cannot present that openly, I am doing the next best thing, which is to compile, organize, streamline and cross-index the voluminous circumstantial evidence. In order to stick (as closely as this radical subject matter may allow) to conventionally accepted factoids, I use boilerplate citations from the USA Wikipedia for historical context and technical reference wherever possible. Wikipedia is not an infallible oracle, but as an orthodox sampling of 'received' opinion on most of the topics I treat, it's a good-enough point of departure.

Even when I have incorporated pre-existing skeptical material, I have developed my own cross-correlated and creatively annotated versions of those (usually inchoate and underdeveloped) points. I don't cite sources for those kinds of random internet inspirations, partly because of the *identity* problem. Most internet boosters and drive-by cheerleaders for the null nukes conjecture use aliases, handles and nicknames. It's meaningless to credit net handles and nonsense nicknames. Additionally, there's the *provenance* and *origination* issue. Who am I to say Mr. or Ms. X is *the* one to be credited with a specific point of analysis or citation? Everything's being copied back and forth relentlessly. The info flow is as restless and unknowable as the quantum superposition of atomic orbitals.

Introduction: SATAN 2

Ultimately does it matter who first made what little point about which minuscule anomaly? The only unitary and truly original 'smoking gun' out there is the *formula of scientific infeasibility* – and that can't be published. Apart from that, there's no other absolute, final coffin nail to the nuclear orthodoxy. There's only a creeping accretion - preponderance of the evidence. This book is a circumscribed but incrementally convincing compilation of all relevant peripheral evidence and logic.

Throughout the book I'll use *Fake Atomic Instantaneous Liquidation* - with its easy acronym **FAIL** - for the hypothesis that explosive nukes don't work. *Liquidation* might seem a weird term in the technical sense (to refer to the putative adverse effects of atomic explosion), but consider its synonyms: *destruction, eradication, annihilation, murder, extermination, carnage*. The end of the world as we know it - *not*. The FAIL hypothesis holds that nuclear weapons are a technical fizzle rebranded for super-sized shock and awe, not to mention a triumph of political/social command and control.

The book eases you gently into this radioactive retention pond, or no - more like a tropical lagoon. Picture the gentle lapping of warm azure wavelets on a South Seas coral atoll… Certainly no sane person would associate nuclear hellfire with that sweet paradise. So you'll hardly notice that, as the book drills forward, you now seem to be out on the ocean side of the reef and the waves are big and dark, and hitting harder, and the spray is biting now, and the ocean floor is falling away beneath your feet as you can't wade any deeper while the tide is ripping you out to sea. And the book will continue to build as we dive deeper, to the point where the conventional nuke story is being clamped and crushed on all sides by so many atmospheres that the hull begins to creak and groan, and rivets start popping from the inner seams like a .50 cal. fusillade across the control room. Climb aboard for a wild ride.

In no area of modern life is the chasm separating experts from lay readers wider than when it comes to nuclear weapons. This is both by deliberate design (national security laws), and by natural tendency (the topic is too complex and depressing for most people to even approach). This book is an inevitably insufficient and limited treatment of the world's most complicated and urgent problem. I hope it will serve as a fire-striker to spark up radical inquiry.

Fire Last Time

Fear porn has a long and distinguished history. India's epic saga, the *Mahabharata* (BCE), perhaps the greatest story ever told, wows the reader with the doomsday weapons of the gods – the *Brahmastra* and *Brahmashira* (literally 'God-head') missiles. The ancient writings, when paired with their counterparts in modern-day nuclear documents and doctrine, sound like shouts and echoes mirroring each other across the same chasm of time.

Nuclear Missiles:

> *Then the descendant of Kakutstha, taking out of his quiver an excellent arrow furnished with handsome wings and golden feathers and a bright and beautiful head, fixed it on the bow with Brahmastra mantra.*
>
> (Mahabharata)

Missiles using a ballistic trajectory usually deliver a warhead over the horizon, at distances of thousands of kilometers, as in the case of intercontinental ballistic missiles (ICBMs) and submarine-launched ballistic missiles (SLBMs). Most ballistic missiles exit the Earth's atmosphere and re-enter it in their sub-orbital spaceflight.

(Wikipedia)

Arming a Nuclear Weapon:

And beholding that excellent arrow, transformed by Rama with proper mantras into a Brahma weapon, the celestials and the Gandharvas with Indra at their head, began to rejoice. And the gods and the Danavas and the Kinnaras were led by the display of that Brahma weapon to regard the life of their Rakshasa foe almost closed.

(Mahabharata)

By way of definition, the arming system of a nuclear weapon is that portion of the weapon which originates the signals required to arm, safe, or re-safe the firing and fuzing systems, and to actuate the nuclear safing system. ... Currently, as many as six different types of safety devices are used together in a single warhead to prevent inadvertent nuclear detonation. Arming may also be accomplished by a single high energy electrical pulse generator when a weapon is released from its delivery vehicle.

('The Swords of Armageddon: U.S. Nuclear Weapons Development since 1945' Chuck Hansen)

Incineration and Vaporization:

Then Rama shot that terrible weapon of unrivalled energy, destined to compass Ravana's death, and resembling the curse of a Brahmana on the point of utterance. And as soon, O Bharata, as that arrow was shot by Rama from his bow drawn to a circle, the Rakshasa king with his chariot and charioteer and horses blazed up, surrounded on all sides by a terrific fire. And deprived of universal dominion by the energy of the Brahma weapon, the five elements forsook the illustrious Ravana. And were consumed by the Brahma weapon, the physical ingredients of Ravana's body. His flesh and blood were all reduced to nothingness - so that the ashes even could not be seen.

(Mahabharata – from the partial retelling of Ramayana)

Death Object

Intense infrared energy is released and instantly burns exposed skin for miles in every direction. The soft internal organs (viscera) of humans and animals are evaporated. Nuclear shadows appear for the first time as a result of the extreme thermal radiation. These shadows are outlines of humans and objects that blocked the thermal radiation. Examples are the woman who was sitting on the stairs near the bank of the Ota River. Only the shadow of where she sat remains in the concrete. The shadow of a man pulling a cart across the street is all that remains in the asphalt.

(Atomic Heritage Foundation)

'... *his flesh and blood were all reduced to nothingness*' A Hiroshima 'nuclear shadow' of one or more vaporized victims (Why is the wood wall unscathed? Just ... don't ask).

Intellectual Pride:

> *Witness today my feats. Behold today my excellent weapons, my Brahmastra and other celestial weapons, as also those that are human. I shall, by my mind alone, hurl today at Partha, for my victory, that weapon of immeasurable energy, called the Brahmastra. ... Savyasaci of immeasurable soul bowed unto Brahman and invoked into existence that excellent irresistible weapon called Brahmastra, which could be applied by the mind alone.*
>
> (Mahabharata)

I have felt it myself. The glitter of nuclear weapons. It is irresistible if you come to them as a scientist. To feel it's there in your hands, to release this energy that fuels the stars, to let it do your bidding. To perform these miracles, to lift a million tons of rock into the sky. It is something that gives people an illusion of illimitable power, and it is, in some ways, responsible for all our troubles — this, what you might call technical arrogance, that overcomes people when they see what they can do with their minds.

(Freeman Dyson)

Wind Blast:

> *The Suta's son then, for slaying the son of Pandu, took up a terrible arrow blazing like fire. When that adored shaft was fixed on the bowstring, the earth, O king, trembled with her mountains and waters and forests. Violent winds began to blow, bearing hard pebbles. All the points of the compass became enveloped with dust.*
>
> (Mahabharata)

'Little Boy' also created ultra high pressure. The wind speed on the ground directly beneath the explosion was believed to have been 980 mph and this speed generated a pressure the equivalent to 8,600 lbs per square feet. One third of a mile from the bomb blast, the wind speed was thought to be 620 mph which created a pressure of 4,600 lbs per square feet. One mile from the centre of the blast, the wind speed was still 190 mph and this speed created a pressure the equivalent of 1,180 lbs per square feet.

(History Learning Site)

Mushroom Cloud:

The earth seemed to tremble with loud sounds of wailing. Then the thick dust, raised by the wind resembling a canopy of tawny silk, enveloped the sky and the sun.

(Mahabharata)

Within another 20 seconds or so the cloud started to push up through the undercast. It first appeared as a parachute which was being blown up by a large electric fan. After the hemispherical cap had emerged through the cloud layer one could see a cloud of smoke about 1/3 the diameter of the "parachute" connecting the bottom of the hemisphere with the undercast. This had very much the appearance of a large mushroom.

(Luis Alvarez – Trinity nuclear test eyewitness)

Panic and Total Destruction

A thick gloom suddenly shrouded the (Pandava) host. All the points of the compass also were enveloped by that darkness. Inauspicious winds began to blow. The sun himself no longer gave any heat. Clouds roared in the welkin, showering blood. The very elements seemed to be perturbed. The sun seemed to turn. The universe, scorched with heat, seemed to be in a fever. The elephants and other creatures of the land, scorched by the energy of that weapon, ran in fright, breathing heavily and desirous of protection against that terrible force. The very waters heated, the creatures residing in that element, O Bharata, became exceedingly uneasy and seemed to burn. From all the points of the compass, cardinal and subsidiary, from the firmament and the very earth, showers of sharp and fierce arrows fell and issued with the impetuosity of Garuda or the wind. Struck and burnt by those shafts of Ashwathama that were all endued with the impetuosity of the thunder, the hostile warriors fell down like trees burnt down by a raging fire. Huge elephants, burnt by that weapon, fell down on the earth all around, uttering fierce cries loud as the rumblings of the clouds. Other huge elephants, scorched by that fire, ran hither and thither, and roared aloud in fear, as if in the midst of a forest conflagration. The steeds, O king, and the cars also, burnt by the energy of that weapon, looked, O sire, like the tops of trees burnt in a forest-fire. Thousands of cars fell down on all sides. Indeed, O Bharata, it seemed that the divine lord Agni burnt the (Pandava) host in that battle, like the Samvarta fire - consuming everything at the end of the Age.

(Mahabharata)

A huge fireball formed in the sky. Directly beneath it is Matsuyama township. Together with the flash came the heat rays and blast, which instantly destroyed everything on earth, and those in the area fell unconscious and were crushed to death. Then they were blown up in the air and hurled back to the ground. The roaring flames burned those caught under the structures who were crying or groaning for help. When the fire burnt itself out, there appeared a completely changed, vast, colorless world that made you think it was the end of life on earth. In a heap of ashes lay the debris of the disaster and charred trees, presenting a gruesome scene. The whole city became extinct. Citizens who were in Matsuyama township, the hypocenter, were all killed instantly, excepting a child who was in an air-raid shelter.

('Record of the Nagasaki A-bomb War Disaster')

Mutual Assured Destruction, Nuclear Ethics, Nuclear Winter:

That region where the weapon called Brahmashira is baffled by another high weapon suffers a drought for twelve years, for the clouds do not pour a drop of water there for this period. For this reason, the mighty-armed son of Pandu, although he had the power, would not, from desire of doing good to living creatures, baffle thy weapon with his. The Pandavas should be protected; thy own self should be protected; the kingdom also should be protected. Therefore, O thou of mighty arms, withdraw this celestial weapon of thine. Dispel this wrath from thy heart and let the Pandavas be safe. The royal sage Yudhisthira never desires to win victory by perpetrating any sinful act! The weapon called Brahmashira, which that subjugator of hostile towns, Drona, communicated to his son, is capable of consuming the whole world. The illustrious and highly blessed preceptor, that foremost of all wielders of bows, delighted with Dhananjaya, had given him that very weapon. Unable to endure it, his only son then begged it of him. Unwillingly he imparted the knowledge of that weapon to Ashvatthama. The illustrious Drona knew the restlessness of his son. Acquainted with all duties, the preceptor laid this command on him, saying, "Even when overtaken by the greatest danger, O child in the midst of battle, thou shouldst never use this weapon, particularly against human beings."

(Mahabharata)

The MAD doctrine assumes that each side has enough nuclear weaponry to destroy the other side and that either side, if attacked for any reason by the other, would retaliate without fail with equal or greater force. The expected result is an immediate, irreversible escalation of hostilities resulting in both combatants' mutual, total, and assured destruction.

(Wikipedia)

Not to be outdone, even the Christian Bible chimes in on this theme:

> *But the day of the Lord will come as a thief in the night; in which the heavens shall pass away with a great noise, and the elements shall melt with fervent heat, the earth also and the works that are therein shall be burned up.*
>
> *Seeing then that all these things shall be dissolved, what manner of persons ought ye to be in all holy conversation and godliness, looking for and hasting unto the coming of the day of God, wherein the heavens being on fire shall be dissolved, and the elements shall melt with fervent heat?*

(2 Peter 3:10 - 12)

What if some halfwit were to assert that the above kinds of ancient nuke-speak are *prima facie* evidence of the *actual* existence of pre-20th century nuclear weapons? The immediate reaction from any rational, intelligent, educated, analytical person would be: *bullshit*. Logical intellects, confronted with this set of cherry-picked quote pairings in support of any such ridiculous contention, would immediately set about debunking the idiotic claim of 'ancient nukes'. They'd drill furiously into stuff like the presumed technological levels of the ancient societies, the lack of physical evidence, the likely motives of the kings and scribes, and so on. After all, those writings were mere fantasy scripts crafted by a dominant priesthood to maintain control through fear and mystification. To that I say: *Go get 'em, champ*! That's exactly the mindset we need. You'd be making my argument for me.

Fire This Time

We must formulate the *Fake Atomic Instantaneous Liquidation* (FAIL) hypothesis very carefully. Taking the time upfront to sculpt the FAIL correctly can save infinite irrelevant counter-argumentative keystrokes when the FAIL takes the field against its many doubters, mockers, scoffers, debunkers and defenders of orthodoxy. A carefully bounded FAIL is also a lot easier to talk about.

The entire focus of the FAIL is the word 'weapons': nuclear *weapons* do not function. This says nothing about nuclear power, as in power plants or submarine engines. Presumably, it is possible to generate electric power via slow and controlled nuclear fission reactions, which generate heat for steam turbines. Perhaps some skeptics would take issue with even that limited claim, but I'm not one of those.

Clearly nuclear power generation is possible and maybe useful (if the safety and waste issues can be handled). Here I'm looking solely at the putative phenomenon of uncontrolled nuclear chain reactions that release a massive charge of atomic 'binding energy' in nanoseconds, vaporizing everything in sight. Counter-arguments to the FAIL must therefore also focus entirely on rapid, uncontrolled nuclear chain reactions deployed for military purposes. It's no use counter-attacking FAIL by citing the reality of nuclear power generation. I'm likewise side-stepping any position, pro or con, on nuclear power safety issues. Nuclear power plants and nuclear power generation will be cited only when relevant to radiation and fallout from nuclear weapons.

This book doesn't attempt a full review of the orthodox standard narrative - the claim that *explosive nukes exist and function as specified*. For convenience let's call that the FEAR (*Functional Explosive Atomic Reality* or if you prefer, the more common spellout: *False Evidence Appearing Real*) hypothesis. FEAR is so widely promulgated, supported, and bolstered on all sides that it needs no further spotlight. Every sane, educated, rational, informed adult citizen of the world feels nuclear FEAR implicitly and wholeheartedly. Only a total idiot would doubt it. Rather than lay out the entire accepted history and theory of nuclear weapons, I will cherry-pick aspects of the conventional story as needed, when I require a foil to make my point. I always attempt to state the orthodox positions in as fair and balanced a way as possible, thus giving **FEAR** every sporting chance.

Born Secret

Those of us who saw the dawn of the Atomic Age that early morning at Alamogordo know now that when man is willing to make the effort, he is capable of accomplishing virtually anything.

General Leslie Richard Groves

Enemy At the Gates

Here we are, 70+ years on from July 16, 1945. Mankind hasn't changed. The philosopher Santayana opined that *only the dead have seen the end of war*. That hasn't changed either. So, up to our ears in super-weapons, you'd think we'd be nuking each other left and right by now. Yet it hasn't come to pass. Why?

Some people talk about *materials*. It's too hard to get your hands on uranium ore in the first place, or too hard to enrich it to weapons grade, or to generate plutonium from it. I see that objection and raise you the classic nuclear biography 'The Curve of Binding Energy', published in 1973. Here's a mild and partial sample of author John McPhee's observations:

> *Some months later… it was disclosed that sixty kilograms of U235 was unaccounted for at a nuclear-fuel-fabricating plant in Apollo, Pennsylvania.*
>
> *The development of other methods of isotropic separation has weakened that* [nuclear materials security] *barricade, and there is a possibility that it has broken down altogether.*

> *All the uranium on the near side of the enrichment plant – in the mine, in the mill, in the factory that turns it into [uranium hexafluoride] – may soon be vulnerable to misuse.*
>
> *Where is the more than half a million kilograms of weapons-grade uranium that has been produced in the United States since 1945? Roughly two per cent has been exploded.*
>
> *The amount of plutonium needed for a bomb is a steady figure, whereas the figure for throughput of plutonium-239 in a place like this will go up and up and up.*
>
> ('The Curve of Binding Energy' John McPhee)

We can scoff that this book came out over forty years ago. Nothing to see here. People were Neanderthals back then. But there's a lot more uranium (out of the ground) and plutonium (from reactors) now. It's likely that, although some high-end Potemkin production and storage facilities have been super-hardened since McPhee's book appeared, the far greater quantities of the material produced since then have totally overwhelmed controls.

That's the materials side of it. Other people talk about *secret knowledge*. This is a fork with two tines, founded on these twin assumptions:

(1) The working instructions on how to make a bomb have been well-guarded and everybody's been kept in the dark;

(2) Despite the 'existence proofs' of Trinity, Hiroshima, and Nagasaki (plus the thousands of nuclear tests around the world since then), technical people (outside the Nuclear Club) are too dumb to reverse-engineer a bomb.

Let's deal with these one at a time. Certainly the original wizards of the craft, the United States nuclear weapons establishment, have kept it pretty much under wraps. This is done under the mil.gov's "born secret" doctrine.

> *"Born secret" and "born classified" are both terms which refer to a policy of information being classified from the moment of its inception,*

> usually regardless of where it was being created, usually in reference to information that describes the operation of nuclear weapons. It has been extensively used in reference to the Atomic Energy Act of 1946, which specified that all information about nuclear weapons and nuclear energy was to be considered "Restricted Data" (RD) until it had been officially declassified. The "born secret" policy was created under the assumption that nuclear information could be so important to national security that it would need classification before it could be formally evaluated. The wording specified:
>
> All data concerning (1) design, manufacture, or utilization of atomic weapons; (2) the production of special nuclear material; or (3) the use of special nuclear material in the production of energy.
>
> Whether or not it is constitutional to declare entire categories of information preemptively classified has not been definitively tested in the courts.
>
> (Wikipedia)

Despite this, a lot of stuff has leaked out. The high profile cases like that of Klaus Fuchs (who gave Manhattan Project data to the Soviet Union) are well known. But much has happened below that level of James Bond cloak-and-dagger operations.

Documents with detailed technical specs have been found on the back shelves of public libraries. Encyclopedia articles have revealed the internal architecture of various devices. Data tables of chemical and nuclear properties essential for fine-tuning your nuke have appeared here and there over the years, often under official government imprimatur. By inference from museum exhibits, dimensional scaling from cross-correlated historical photographs, and interviews with old-time nuclear engineers, obsessive amateur nuclear detectives have ferreted out all kinds of engineering specs and process details. These dribs and drabs have in turn been re-packaged and published in any number of openly available books and popular magazine articles. So the secrecy cloak has in practice been a shaggy, baggy, leaky thing. *But the law stands as written.*

Geek-Out

I'm going to assume that you have at least a minimal understanding of basic physics and chemistry. Therefore you know the Rutherford-Bohr model of the atom:

> *In atomic physics, the Rutherford–Bohr model or Bohr model or Bohr diagram, introduced by Niels Bohr and Ernest Rutherford in 1913, depicts the atom as a small, positively charged nucleus surrounded by electrons that travel in circular orbits around the nucleus—similar in structure to the Solar System, but with attraction provided by electrostatic forces rather than gravity.*
>
> (Wikipedia)

Though to a purist this model is technically 'obsolete' (overly simplistic in a number of marginal respects) it's 'good enough for government work' and is commonly taught as the conventional picture we have in our minds:

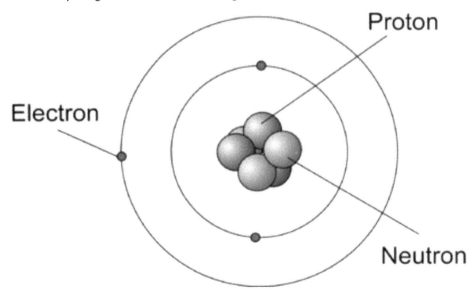

Rutherford-Bohr atomic approximation.

But popular illustrations are wildly out of scale:

> The size of the helium nucleus is about 1 fermi, or 1 fm, which is equivalent to 10-15 m. The atom is about 100,000 times bigger than the nucleus, with an atom size of about 105 fm or 10-10 m.
>
> (NASA's Cosmos)

So if the nucleus above were the size of a baseball, the outer electron shell would be miles of empty space distant from it.

The basic points of the FEAR hypothesis are that:

(a) There exists a tractable configuration of a certain material which neutrons can traverse with a sufficient hit rate on that material's nuclei to break them up, thus propagating a growing nuclear splitting process;

(b) The above can happen at sufficient speed and to a sufficient degree to build up explosive pressure within containment without being impeded or prematurely halted by any other factor.

Pinball as Extinction Level Event

> *A theory that you can't explain to a barmaid is probably no damn good.*
>
> Ernest Rutherford

Explosive fission is, in *some* ways, analogous to the classic game of pinball (in *other* ways… not so much).

> Pinball is a type of arcade game, in which points are scored by a player manipulating one or more steel balls on a play field inside a glass-covered cabinet called a pinball machine (or pinball table). The primary objective of the game is to score as many points as possible. Points are earned when the ball strikes different targets on the play field. A drain

is situated at the bottom of the play field, partially protected by player-controlled plastic bats called flippers. A game ends after all the balls fall into the drain a certain number of times. Secondary objectives are to maximize the time spent playing (by earning "extra balls" and keeping the ball in play as long as possible) and to earn bonus games (known as "replays").

(Wikipedia)

PINBALL	NUCLEAR FISSION
playfield	fissile mass
plunger	initiator
balls	neutrons
target	fissionable nucleus
bumper	neutron scattering
flipper	reflector
drain	neutron leakage
extra balls	supercritical
replay	chain reaction

It also has something in common with pinball's close relative, Pachinko.

In Pachinko, the ball [**neutron**] *enters the playing field* [**fissile mass**], *which is populated by a large number of brass pins* [**nuclei**], *several small cups into which the player hopes the ball will fall* [**fissionable nuclei**] *(each catcher is barely the width of the ball), and a hole at the bottom into which the ball will fall if it doesn't enter a catcher. The ball bounces from pin to pin, both slowing the fall and making it travel laterally across the field. A ball which enters a catcher will trigger a payout* [**delayed neutrons**], *in which a number of balls are dropped into a tray at the front of the machine. The object of the game is to capture as many balls as possible. These balls can then be exchanged for prizes* [**death and destruction on a truly epic scale**].

(Wikipedia)

Binding Energy

There seems to be a little residual unclarity on the nature, source and magnitude of the basic energetic factor. Many people assume that, since a bit of mass is "missing" in measurements of post-fission nuclei, that this missing mass has been converted to energy via Einstein's $e = mc^2$. Here's how Los Alamos nuclear weapons designer Ted Taylor described it:

> *It had to do with binding energy, and it was that when Fat Man exploded over Nagasaki the amount of matter that changed into energy and destroyed the city was one gram – a third the weight of a penny. A number of kilograms of plutonium were in the bomb, but the amount that actually released its binding energy and created the fireball was one gram. E (twenty kilotons) equals m (one gram) times the square of the speed of light.*

> ('The Curve of Binding Energy' John McPhee)

Taylor's summary, if accurate, would also cover the Hiroshima Little Boy bomb, because U235 and plutonium are said to yield close-enough figures per kilogram – about 17,000 tons TNT per kilogram for U235 and about 19,000 for plutonium. As for Einstein's equation, other sober authorities concur with Taylor:

> *After all, $E = mc^2$, which means a very small amount of mass can produce a great amount of energy, given the speed of light.*

> ('High-Powered Lasers Deliver Fusion Energy Breakthrough' Scientific American February 12 2014)

All this contrasts with Robert Serber's account:

> *Somehow the popular notion took hold long ago that Einstein's theory of relativity, in particular his famous equation $E = mc^2$, plays some essential role in the theory of fission. Albert Einstein had a part in*

alerting the United States government to the possibility of building an atomic bomb, but his theory of relativity is not required in discussing fission. The theory of fission is what physicists call a nonrelativistic theory, meaning that relativistic effects are too small to affect the dynamics of the fission process significantly.

('The Los Alamos Primer' Robert Serber)

None of the experts above should be susceptible to any 'popular notion' on such a fundamental point. According to Serber:

The energy released in fission is exactly the same as the origin of the energy released when two atoms or molecules react chemically. It's the electrostatic energy between two similarly charged particles. Two similarly large particles repel each other. There's an electrical force pushing them apart.

Serber uses his own equation to derive the specifics of that electrostatic energy. In a simple case of "electrons pushed together" it appears as:

$$E = e^2 / R$$

where:

e is the electron charge, e^2 is e multiplied by itself, and R is the distance between the particles. The electrostatic energy thus ends up as kinetic energy, the energy of motion.

('The Los Alamos Primer' Robert Serber)

This equation could apply to either electrons "pushed together" (a relatively weak encounter) or, more interestingly for explosive fission, it can be extended to apply to the bound protons of a material like the 235 isotope of (enriched) uranium. In the case of U235, after plugging in the relevant pieces of the equation and running through a few conversions, Serber emerges with an order-of-magnitude (roughly correct) energetic equivalent: 1 kilogram of U235 = 20,000 tons of TNT. There is a bit of formulaic fussiness in that final number. The equivalence is actually somewhere in a range between 10,000 and 20,000 tons of TNT. But basically the Serber formula yields the desired range, matching the "reality" of the Little Boy bomb.

According to Wiki:

> When 1 pound (0.45 kg) of uranium-235 undergoes complete fission, the yield is 8 kilotons. The 16 kiloton yield of the Little Boy bomb was therefore produced by the fission of 2 pounds (0.91 kg) of uranium-235, out of the 141 pounds (64 kg) in the pit.

In other words, when about 1 kilogram of U235 fissions, it gives out the equivalent of 16 kilotons, pretty much in the middle of Serber's range and thus validating his formula. All good. But this shows that something is wrong with the popular understanding of what's really happening in fission. It would be an astonishing coincidence if the (Einstein) equation that crucially relies on, and is largely determined by, the gigantic natural constant c (speed of light at 299,792,458 meters per second, then squared) were able to blindly converge on the 'true' figure as calculated by an entirely unrelated formula that makes no reference to c.

It's interesting that even as authoritative and august a voice as physicist Robert Smyth in his classic work on weaponized nuclear physics ('A General Account of the Development of Methods of Using Atomic Energy for Military Purposes', 1945) falls into this same error of dragging $e = mc^2$ onto the gameboard to account for the blast power of nuclear fission. You'd have imagined that he of all people would have read 'The Los Alamos Primer'.

Probably this popular notion 'took hold' due to the tabloid-style reporting of Manhattan Project embedded sci-fi propagandist William Laurence.

BORN SECRET

William Laurence (left) New York Times embedded atomic fabulist, with Oppenheimer (right) at Trinity test site.

You'd like to think that these confusions will turn out to be merely divergent vocabularies for describing essentially the same thing. Genius mathematician John Von Neumann observed: *"If one has really technically penetrated a subject, things that previously seemed in complete contrast might be purely mathematical transformations of each other."* But in this case, the two explanations are distinct phenomena, whose relation (at the level of nuclear phenomena) is more that of marginal overlap rather than variable terminology for a unitary underlying process. In nuclear reactions, energy and mass are conserved separately.

Something is being fudged somewhere. But that's ok. It's not a demonic conspiracy, just a little misunderstanding common to the editors of popular books and websites. The conversion of mass to energy in fission is merely being hugely over-emphasized, distorted and misrepresented. It's perfectly all right to have different levels of sophistication and correspondingly more or less precise terms of description. As long as no *real* nuclear expert, no *professional Los Alamos lab weapons designer*, would make the mistake of using the relativity equation to derive the energy output and the TNT equivalence… Oh wait… there's Taylor's account of fission energy, quoted above. The point is that even the most scientific-sounding numbers and explanatory formulae can turn out to be fudged and wrongly applied, whether by guile, carelessness, or ignorance.

Stonewall

I'd love to drag you into the weeds with me at this point. We could have a serious geekfest crunching through all the technical data on the exact specs of the (supposed) explosive fission process. But we now hit a technical and conceptual stonewall. The graffiti scrawled across that wall names the problem: *explosive fast fission*. Ignoring a huge mass of detail, the situation is that for explosive fission to occur:

- enough 'fast' (high energy) **neutrons** need to …
- hit enough **targets** (fissionable nuclei) within …
- a short enough **time**.

There are many levels of neutron 'speed' (energy), many ways in which the 'speed' can be affected or controlled, and many ways the targets may be presented or arranged. The result is a large combinatory space, which spans various kinds of nuclear reactor technologies and atomic bomb configurations.

An explosive process by definition requires speed. For that, you have to work with high energy *fast neutrons*. The downside is that fast neutrons are, all else equal, less likely than slow neutrons to hit a target nucleus in the fissionable material. So you have to tweak other levers and switches to retain the advantage of fast neutrons (*speed of resulting reaction*) while minimizing their disadvantage (*less likely to hit anything*).

> *It's not easy to get a neutron to hit the nucleus. Think of it! It's like shooting a bullet into memorial stadium and trying to hit that mosquito. Most of the time you miss.*
>
> (Professor Richard Muller, UC Berkeley)

Typical tweaks include:

- *Enrichment* of the fissionable material: Provide nuclei that are most likely to fission easily when encountered. For weapons, this means using enriched U235 uranium isotope (derived from natural U238 via various chemical and/or electromagnetic processes) or plutonium (derived from U238 via slow fission in a reactor, followed by chemical separation).
- *More neutrons:* Plutonium has the edge over U235 in this department, releasing on average 2 to 3 neutrons per fission event vs. 1 to 2 neutrons for U235. You can also increase neutrons by using a good initiator that sprays out a lot of them right at the start of critical assembly, or even by using fusion of hydrogen isotopes as a layer in a device, which creates a big neutron spray.
- *Shaping* of the fissionable material: All else equal, a sphere is considered optimal for keeping the neutrons bounded within a geometry presenting minimal surface area.
- *Reflection* of neutrons: The critical mass of fissionable material can be encased in layers of something that prevents neutrons from leaking out of the reaction, into the surroundings where they no longer contribute to the fission.
- *Compression* of the fissionable material, creating a denser target field of nuclei. This means contriving to mash the fissile mass into itself, (commonly accomplished with an enclosing shell of high explosives focused inward onto a sphere of fissionable material).

The pre-bang checklist requires incredibly elaborate and precise calculations to insure that a sufficient _quantity_ of fast neutrons, going at 'fast' enough _speeds_ as they blast through the material, are _likely_ enough to hit a target nucleus, with a high enough proportion of those encounters of the right _type_ (breaking apart the target nucleus rather than being captured by it or any of a number of other possible sub-optimal outcomes) resulting in enough neutrons being _liberated_ in the collisions to propagate the process onward. And, most crucially, that all this will happen in just the right amount of _time_ for an explosive outcome. It's a real Goldilocks problem because the target nuclei are few and far between, given the atomic scale facts covered at the start of this section.

I don't mean to shirk the hard labor of stepping through all the analytical details and unraveling how or whether 'they' (the past and current bomb scientists) got all the stuff above just right. But now a *conceptual* roadblock rears up against us. It's a fundamental tenet of science that results are described openly, in sufficient detail for replication by skilled readers. But for safety reasons this standard protocol doesn't apply to nukes. And the tight security leaves us with no way to probe the truth and resolve the workability of these claims… right?

The Nuclear Secret That Dare Not Speak Its Name

'But the whole universe is outside us. Look at the stars! Some of them are a million light-years away. They are out of our reach for ever.'

'What are the stars?' said O'Brien indifferently. 'They are bits of fire a few kilometres away. We could reach them if we wanted to. Or we could blot them out. The earth is the centre of the universe. The sun and the stars go round it.'

'1984' George Orwell

Let's zero right in on the matter at hand:

The object of the project is to produce a practical military weapon in the form of a bomb in which the energy is released by a fast neutron chain reaction in one or more of the materials known to show nuclear fission.

('The Los Alamos Primer' Robert Serber)

That was the goal, and if FEAR is believed, the result of the Manhattan Project, running (for my purposes) from 1943 through mid-1945. Did it really happen? Consider the scientific situation:

> *In an enterprise such as the building of the atomic bomb the difference between ideas, hopes, suggestions and theoretical calculations, and solid numbers based on measurement, is paramount. All the committees, the politicking and the plans would have come to naught if a few unpredictable nuclear cross sections had been different from what they are by a factor of two.*
>
> (Emilio Segrè)

Other luminaries had their doubts:

> *Very often we kept saying maybe we'll come across some insuperable physical obstacle, which prevents it from working. You can easily imagine those things. For example, a little delay in the emission of fast neutrons after fission.*
>
> (Phillip Morrison)

Though explosive fission seems so blatantly obvious now, there's no *a priori* reason why the power of fission should be harvestable in any manner, for electricity or bombs. Given the range of possible ways the world could be, it's actually rather unlikely and amazing that the numbers happen to work perfectly to enable this useful technology. It's wrong to assume that unbounded human ingenuity can make anything at all happen.

Burn the Sky!

Consider a counter-example, an opposite counterpart to the miracle of the 'just so' numbers that make explosive fission (seem) possible. Nature simply turns thumbs down on another attractive doomsday idea, early speculation about setting the atmosphere on fire:

> *Edward* [Teller] *brought up the notorious question of igniting the atmosphere. Bethe went off in his usual way, put in the numbers, and showed that it couldn't happen. It was a question that had to be answered but it never was anything, it was a question only for a few hours. It somehow got into a document that went to Washington. So every once in a while after that, someone happened to notice it, and then back down the ladder came the question, and the thing never was laid to rest.*
>
> ('The Los Alamos Primer' Robert Serber)

So it's amazing – in one case, the numbers didn't happen to work out (to allow for igniting the entire atmosphere) and in another case they did – for nuclear fission, which, when worked, reworked, amplified and turned inside out enables a doomsday machine that indeed could destroy the earth in another way. So, who are you going to believe? Suppose that a big team of geniuses were to be given the military mission: *create a doomsday weapon that can ignite the atmosphere.* Would they have eventually triumphed over nature, would they have broken through the barrier of Bethe's "*numbers* [which] *showed that it couldn't happen*"? Some things just don't work. Explosive nuclear fission is one of those things, and the interesting questions are *when* its infeasibility was discovered and *how* that fact was handled.

Virtual Manhattan Project

> *With four parameters I can fit an elephant, and with five I can make him wiggle his trunk.*
>
> - John von Neumann

The ultimate mystery about nukes is why, after all these years, from 1946 on, *nobody* has ever nuked *anybody* in anger (if you're reading this by the glow of a green glass parking lot, you may be forgiven a sardonic chuckle). Maybe the doctrine of Mutual Assured Destruction really is restraining the bloodlust. But the MAD doctrine only applies to nations. National leaders obviously care nothing for the lives in their charge, but they are attached to their palaces and limos. The politicians' uncertainty as to whether those perks could be up and running quickly enough after a nuke exchange is enough to restrain them - for now. But that doesn't apply to terrorists who are happy to die for The Cause. So then the question arises of why no terrorist bad guys have yet nuked anything. The usual answer boils down to lack of these components:

- Materials
- Knowledge
- Infrastructure

It's assumed that those resources are a 'bridge too far' for a terrorist organization. The usual show-stopper statement to avoid the whole topic is: "*You'd need another Manhattan Project.*" I could go deeply into all the contradictions and absurdities that abound on this subject. But in this section, I want to discuss whether the FEAR hypothesis is valid.

Given all the restrictions on publicizing the science and design factors that enable explosive fission, it seems we've struck out on the 'replication' requirement that underlies real science. It appears that all anybody can do it accept spoon-feeding of filmed results and expert testimony. But appearances deceive. There *is* a way that the validity of explosive fission could be verified. The method outlined in this book is only a thought experiment. It involves no acquisition or use of fissionable materials whatsoever. It is proffered strictly in the service of the search for truth.

It must however be said that, sadly, there is no barrier preventing a small group of bad guys, not to mention a nation or sophisticated criminal organization from doing in *reality* what is outlined here as mere *virtuality*. And the horrible beauty of the scheme is that, by the precedent of the Manhattan Project, the development procedure sketched here is *guaranteed to work*.

Is there only enough fissionable material for a single bomb? No problem. By following the procedure here, bad guys could develop a nuclear weapon that works perfectly on first firing – *without testing*. No classified information would need to be accessed. It is thus the fabled 'unclassified bomb'. All that's needed is one bomb's worth of fissionable material. I'll cover the materials issue elsewhere. Now, let's talk about the knowledge problem and the design challenge for building a 21st century unclassified bomb. If the FEAR hypothesis is correct, this procedure cannot fail to produce a working weapon.

Consider the original Manhattan Project. Forget about the materials problem for a moment (General Groves is on it). The Los Alamos scientists began with a theory and a goal, nothing more. The theory told them that explosive fission should be possible. As far as post-1945 conventional scientific thought is concerned, this theory is true. It was fully validated at Trinity, Hiroshima, and Nagasaki.

So how did they get from their true theory to their realized goal? In terms of anything remotely recognizable today as serious simulation they had only Stone Age tools. They relied on pure brains and instinct, just a wing and prayer. They were like the pinball wizard in the rock opera *Tommy*, who though deaf, dumb and blind "plays by sense of smell". Because their theory was true, they were able to develop two different weapon designs and implementations, both of which worked perfectly on the very first full test/use (Trinity and Hiroshima). In achieving this, they did all the heavy lifting for all time. The task of today's unclassified bomb builder is *infinitely* simpler and easier than what the Manhattan Project faced in the day. The two challenges should not even be compared.

The Virtual Manhattan Project is built around two essential elements, neither of which was available to the original guys.

1. A reverse-engineered component model.
2. Simulation technology.

With those, it is now possible for, on the one hand, any regular Joe to recruit some friends and build a basement nuke, or on the other hand (more to this book's purpose) to either verify or debunk the FEAR hypothesis.

The Coster-Mullen Component Model

In technology one sometimes hears about 'reverse engineering'.

> ***Reverse engineering****, also called **back engineering**, is the process of extracting knowledge or design information from anything man-made and re-producing it or re-producing anything based on the extracted information.*
>
> (Wikipedia)

An engineer begins with a fully functional example of a working artifact (anything from an electric toothbrush to a software application) and then figures out what makes it tick by inference based on (i) its performance and/or (ii) disassembly for direct inspection.

An analyst has reverse-engineered the first atomic bombs. John Coster-Mullen's book 'Atom Bombs: The Top Secret Inside Story of Little Boy and Fat Man' is a nearly complete design manual for understanding and replicating the simplest original nukes. The book explains every design element and how they all hang together, based on exhaustive review of original documentation and interviews with surviving principals, including scientists, engineers, and military deployment personnel – virtually anyone who had some hand in working on or with the bombs.

C-M's work has been praised to the skies by heavyweight atomic authorities, including former heads of the USA nuclear weapons laboratories, as the only accurate design analysis of the early nukes. Some have even gone so far as to suggest he's in violation of national secrecy laws. But everything in the book was derived from unclassified public reference materials harvested by C-M's laser eyes (poring over hundreds of piecemeal physical prototypes and museum pieces) and his razor logic (applied to establishing connections, catching contradictions and filling in gaps). C-M is clearly the greatest 'reverse engineer' of all time. 'Atom Bombs' is *the how-to manual for the 'unclassified bomb'* that Los Alamos weapons designer Ted Taylor obsessed about in 'The Curve of Binding Energy' (John McPhee).

So then why, apart from the few insider grumbles mentioned above (which Coster-Mullen proudly reproduces in the front matter of his book as testimony to authenticity) hasn't there been more outcry? Why hasn't Coster-Mullen been spirited away by Men In Black, the book scrubbed from Amazon, and all copies flushed down the Orwellian memory hole? Well, for one thing the USA is still a free country, sort of. After all, the book does not reproduce classified documents or include any illegal information found only in such sources.

But the most important reason for the official tolerance extended to this book is the bogus refrain we've heard along: *You'd (still) need another Manhattan Project*. But if the FAIL hypothesis is true - if explosive fission is for real - then that response is a tragic misreading of the situation.

Once possessed of C-M's manual, why (under conventional thinking) might you *still* need another Manhattan Project to produce your unclassified bomb? One thing is the usual sidetrack about fissionable materials. That's not my main focus in this section, but suffice it to say again: read 'The Curve of Binding Energy'. This decades-old book will bleach your hair as you learn how easily bad guys of that time could have possessed themselves of all manner of nasty stuff, including U235 and plutonium, in various forms. Whatever tightening of security and accounting protocols was imposed after the book's appearance has probably been more than out-run and end-run by the huge accumulation of such materials in the ensuing decades – especially outside the USA.

For now, let's put the materials thing aside and concentrate on the weapon's design and function. Decades before C-M's detailed design manual was available, Los Alamos weapons designer Ted Taylor had this to say about the 'unclassified nuke'. It's what I'm talking about here, a proof-of-concept device:

> *Ted Taylor would like to see Los Alamos or Livermore build and detonate a crude, coarse, unclassified nuclear bomb – unclassified in that nothing done in the bomb's fabrication would draw on knowledge that is secret. ... Taylor's instructions to Los Alamos would be "Lay off any sophistication altogether. Try to see how sloppy you can get. Then set the thing off underground. Measure the yield. Put a stop to speculation about this subject."*
>
> ('The Curve of Binding Energy' John McPhee)

As far as anybody knows, this has never been done. The formulaic response from sophisticated readers to the Taylor challenge above has always been, again: *You'd need your own Manhattan Project.* In addition to the C-M manual, there are plentiful public materials to be found in odd places such as the former Encyclopedia Americana, including things like:

> *...factors of density that could be reached in metallic fissile material with certain levels of implosive force*
>
> ('The Curve of Binding Energy' John McPhee)

Put it all together and you have the blueprint of a bomb. I am most emphatically *not* suggesting any non-scientist, people working with a nefarious purpose, should pursue this. Why would you want to hurt anybody? Be a lover, not a fighter. No, the purpose of this excursion is to consider whether there's any way to verify the truth or falsity of the FAIL hypothesis short of physically blowing something up. A thought experiment, if you will.

It turns out there is. And due to the Manhattan Project's (supposed) existence proof, it's now way easier than anything that team faced in the 1940's. All you need is a MacBook. Maybe a MacBook Pro.

Parameter Fitting

Given all the existing materials, the C-M manual and all the rest that's out there, it would be straightforward to construct a functional software simulation of a nuclear weapon. Before anybody freaks out and starts sputtering about super computers and irreducible complexity and so on, listen calmly to exactly what I'm laying down here.

A simulation is built from these points of information:

1. Components, with their *a priori* characteristic and specifications
2. Spatial arrangement of the components
3. Process model of temporal operation

4. Control parameters for the components, their interactions, and their environment
5. A set of workable values for each control parameter

What in the above list is missing or secret at this point? The C-M manual totally covers 1 and 2 and most of 3, certainly for the Little Boy uranium 'gun' type of bomb. The combination of the C-M manual with the essential theory of explosive fission (basic level - *only* what the Manhattan scientists began with) specifies the required parameter types. A starting list of parameter types for core nuke processes would include environmental, characteristic and control factors like these usual suspects (mixing bomb types just to give the idea):

- Type, amount, quality, density, geometry etc. of the fissile mass, including figures for likelihood of fission, neutron capture, average neutrons released per fission, etc.
- Specifications for initiator (neutron source) if any
- Specifications for neutron reflector if any
- Speed and required force of critical assembly mechanism

… and many more. In a practical simulation there might be hundreds of components and processes, each with dozens of parameters and a vast interaction space. All these would be embedded under a physics model, specifying all real-world stuff that might affect the reactions, such as gravity, temperature, magnetic or electric fields, moisture – anything that affects or constrains the intended process. That support piece would be like the high-end 'physics model' used in sophisticated video games. Embedded within the bomb model would be the critical assembly simulator. (I'm not talking about a graphical simulator here. The graphics of this simulation don't matter. We're building a 'good enough' proof-of-concept where all the numbers play well together; reflect the perfectly smooth match between theory and practice demonstrated by the Manhattan Project; and add up to BOOM.)

This isn't eye candy – pretty colors on the screen where you could set any values you want for atom count, neutron count, implosion depth etc. Those are toys. What I'm talking about here is expressing the theoretic elements of explosive fission thoroughly and accurately enough in our parameters such that the model's process when 'run' yields the same explosive numbers that would be reflected in a perfect instrument capture of an actual event such as Trinity. To do that you can't just provide some inputs and not worry about the real world accuracy of the outputs, nor can you set desired outputs and blithely assume the real world feasibility of the generating process and initial conditions. Both ends must match up, just as they did in the Trinity test (I'm talking about the abstract quality of *consistent and realistic modeling*, not about matching the observed values of any one particular test. Any simulation based on input of good theory, expressed in realistic parameter settings, that yields output of the observed values of a real world explosive detonation would qualify as a good simulation.)

That'd be a real hairball of a simulation for sure. That's why the contemporary designers of actual nuclear weapons are so into massive supercomputers. Consider this news story from a few years back:

> LIVERMORE, CALIF. — *A group of nuclear weapons designers and scientists at the Lawrence Livermore National Laboratory conducted a what-if experiment several years ago, deploying supercomputers to simulate what happens to a nuclear weapon from the moment it leaves storage to the point when it hits a target.*
>
> *They methodically worked down a checklist of all the possible conditions that could affect the B-83 strategic nuclear bomb, the most powerful and one of the most modern weapons in the U.S. arsenal, officials said. The scientists and designers examined how temperature, altitude, vibration and other factors would affect the bomb in what is called the stockpile-to-target sequence.*
>
> *Such checks typically have been carried out by taking bombs and warheads apart; scrutinizing them using chemistry, physics, mathematics, materials science and other disciplines; and examining data from earlier nuclear explosive tests. This time, however, the scientists and designers relied entirely on supercomputer modeling, running huge amounts of code.*

> Then came a surprise. The computer simulations showed that at a certain point from stockpile to target, the weapon would "fail catastrophically," according to Bruce T. Goodwin, principal associate director at Livermore for weapons programs. Such a failure would mean that the weapon would not produce the explosive yield expected by the military — either none at all, or something quite different than required to properly hit the target.
>
> (The Washington Post Nov. 1, 2011)

The above report indicates that simulations of complex atomic processes are both feasible and can be functionally reflective of real world outcomes. But the above simulation required some heavy computational lifting, with lots more capacity lined up on the runway for the near future:

> Next May or June, Livermore plans to put into operation an IBM supercomputer, Sequoia, capable of 20 petaflops. A petaflop is a thousand trillion floating point operations per second. The machine, on 96 refrigerator-size racks, will contain 1.6 million processing cores and will be 10 times faster than what is now the fastest computer in the world. By comparison, all the computing power at Livermore today is about 2.5 petaflops.
>
> (Post article)

With these kinds of sophistication and power requirements, how can I assert that a simulation performed with lesser hardware and software capability is even remotely feasible? Consider the situation that has obtained from the time of Trinity until just recently:

> In recent years, physicists at Livermore surmounted one of the oldest and most difficult challenges they faced. In many nuclear weapons explosive tests, measurements suggested that the detonating bombs appeared to violate a law of physics, "conservation of energy," which

> states that in a closed system, the total amount of energy remains constant, and thus energy cannot be either created or destroyed. For decades, the nuclear weaponeers puzzled over why the test results appeared to break from this principle. Then, the "energy balance" problem, as it was known, was solved by a Livermore physicist, Omar Hurricane, who won the 2009 E.O. Lawrence Award from the Department of Energy for his work, which remains classified.
>
> (Post article)

Say *what*?? You have got to be effing kidding me. You mean those early nuclear geniuses, the baddest-ass scientists ever, who got the bomb blowing up first time out, homerun on their first at-bat, with essentially zero system testing, *didn't understand why it worked*? They were flying blind? That's what the above statement appears to suggest, at least for the early hydrogen bombs. A Soviet physicist recalls what he heard about this early uncertainty:

> At a conference at Los Alamos in April 1946, where Teller presented the results of his calculations of Classical Super, Bethe made a remark, that the amount of inverse Compton scattering of γ's (not accounted for by Teller), will result in negative energy balance and that the hydrogen bomb of this type will not explode. In our calculations after hard work we came to the same conclusion – the energy balance was negative.
>
> (Boris Ioffe, Moscow Institute of Theoretical and Experimental Physics)

Well, that's ok. We can take a tolerant view. After all, did the Wright Brothers totally understand all of aviation science when they got their gadget off the ground? It's possible they never even heard of the Bernoulli effect (which may not even be the true/full explanation for aviation 'lift' anyway). And Darwin didn't know about DNA (though he never tried to clone sheep either). Regardless, we have to admire the original atomic gangsters even more – truly they were real-life embodiments of the blind pinball wizard, with *crazy flipper fingers* and *such a supple wrist*.

At least the Wright Brothers were able to do wind test and other engineering integration testing, step by step. But even powered flight is way simpler than building an atomic bomb that works first time out. You have to admire the Manhattan Project's achievement:

- Wrong, confused, or poorly understood theory
- Dozen or hundreds of control and sequencing parameters estimated 'manually'
- No integration testing prior to first major demonstration

At this point we could drag out the tired cliché about *'the probability that a tornado ripping through a junkyard will spontaneously assemble a 747'*. But you won't catch *me* saying that. Because you don't need monster arrays of 20 petaflop machines to do the parameter setting for your working bomb.

All you need is:

1. primitive-but-workable Manhattan Project level of theory
2. some public domain data tables
3. C-M's model of components, layout and process
4. a decent laptop computer
5. Matlab and/or Microsoft Azure and/or Google Cloud and/or any other standard machine learning tools suite

With the above in hand, you can reverse-engineer the one remaining necessary item – the final classified 'secret sauce' of the Trinity, Hiroshima, and Nagasaki bombs – *the parameter settings*. I'm using the term 'parameter setting' in a broad sense for anything variable in the device such as amount and quality of core materials, dimensions of everything, timing, and all else that needs to be numerically specified or controlled.

This is where those who are complacent about books like C-M's manual and McPhee's work on Ted Taylor are sadly fooling themselves when they say: *"You'd need another Manhattan Project."* One Manhattan Project was enough, and, partly as a result of its 'success', the unclassified bomb designer now has access to all the stuff above. So I can assert the following:

1. There exists an unclassified device model M, characterized by parameter set P, which, when engaged according to parameter value set V, is a functional representation of a working atomic bomb.

1. If a device were built and deployed in accordance with M = P(V) it would explode with the yield of Fat Man or Little Boy (depending which was chosen as the basis for M).

Now you say: *gotcha*! Because it's well enough to claim that, while the Manhattan Project's theory was wrong or seriously incomplete, it is a sufficient basis for a working bomb. And it's all very well to say that an accurate device model and set of timing and control parameters is openly available. But what about the parameter settings? There's your showstopper! You'd need *petaflops* of computing power to resolve those.

No, you wouldn't. Consider how the Manhattan Project worked.

> [One process] *of great interest to Los Alamos was the progress of free neutrons hurtling through a nuclear weapon as it began to explode. As Stanislaw Ulam ... would subsequently note, "Most of the physics at Los Alamos could be reduced to the study of assemblies of particles inter- acting with each other, hitting each other, scattering, sometimes giving rise to new particles." Given the speed, direction, and position of a neutron and some physical constants, physicists could fairly easily compute the probability that it would, during the next tiny fraction of a second, crash into the nucleus of an unstable atom with sufficient force to break it up and release more neutrons in a process known as fission. One could also estimate the likelihood that neutrons would fly out of the weapon entirely, change direction after a collision, or get stuck. But even in the very short time span of a nuclear explosion, these simple actions could be combined in an almost infinite number of sequences, defying even the brilliant physicists and mathematicians gathered at Los Alamos to simplify the proliferating chains of probabilities sufficiently to reach a traditional analytical solution.*

> *The arrival of electronic computers offered an alternative: simulate the progress over time of a series of virtual neutrons representing members of the population released by the bomb's neutron initiator when a conventional explosive compressed its core to form a critical mass and trigger its detonation. Following these neutrons through thousands of random events would settle the question statistically, yielding a set of neutron histories that closely approximated the actual distribution implied by the parameters chosen. If the number of fissions increased over time, then a self-sustaining chain reaction was underway. The chain reaction would end after an instant as the core blew itself to pieces, so the rapid proliferation of free neutrons, measured by a parameter the weapon designers called "alpha," was crucial to the bomb's effectiveness in converting enriched uranium into destructive power.*
>
> *The weapon used on Hiroshima is estimated to have fissioned only about 1 percent of its 141 pounds of highly enriched uranium, leaving bomb designers with a great deal of scope for refinement. Using [probabilistic simulations], the explosive yield of various hypothetical weapon designs could be estimated without using up America's precious stockpiles of weapons-grade uranium and plutonium. This was, in essence, an experimental method within a simulated and much simplified reality.*
>
> ('Nuclear Monte Carlo Simulations 1947-1948' Thomas Haigh)

Thus it's clear that fully functional parameter values can be derived even in the absence of accurate theory and based on incomplete experimental results, just by a powerful sampling and automated simulation. But note the date on that description: 1947 – 1948. Right after the war, Los Alamos began to work with serious digital computers, which, though pitifully slow and buggy, were more like today's architectures than the analog calculators and IBM punch card machines used in the initial (wartime) phase.

In the wartime phase, the calculating machinery was truly Stone Age, yet the scientists arrived at good-enough (BOOM!) workable parameter values, which were subsequently locked up as highest state secrets. But with the materials outlined above, and with the incomparably superior parameter estimation and statistical modeling systems available to anybody today practically for free, that secret sauce of 'known-to- BOOM' parameter settings could be easily recovered and replicated. For our purposes, that would validate the explosive fission FEAR hypothesis. Unfortunately, this process would also serve up to any villain or scumbag who comes along a guaranteed-to-BOOM recipe for a working gadget. I'll have more to say on probabilistic simulation methods later in this chapter.

* * *

The Nuclear Secret That Dare Not Speak Its Name

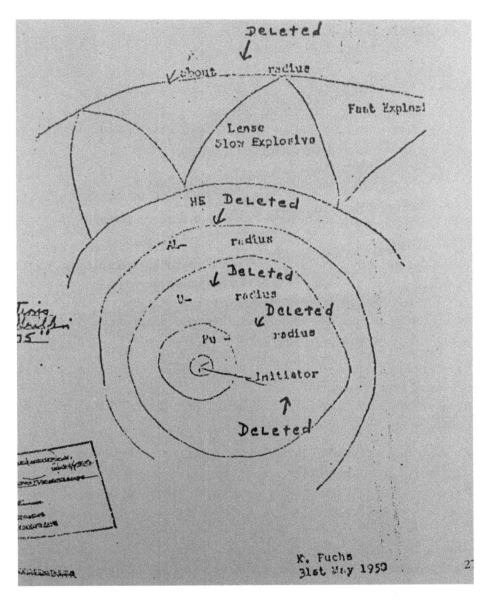

All those 'Deleted' arrows represent numerical parameters, the supposedly 'secret' sauce that separates the sheep of a general layout from the goat of a working device. Given the configuration shown, and a physics model, the parameters can be restored by high-speed simulation. Virtually infinite combinations can be tested and verified in milliseconds.

Checkmate

> *The sciences do not try to explain, they hardly even try to interpret, they mainly make models. By a model is meant a mathematical construct which, with the addition of certain verbal interpretations, describes observed phenomena. The justification of such a mathematical construct is solely and precisely that it is expected to work.*
>
> - John von Neumann

As we've seen in the previous chapter, *timing is everything*. Three things need to happen very quickly:

Assembly: Sub-critical pieces or densities of fissionable material must be kept in sufficient proximity such that they can be put together rapidly in a weapon, yet far enough apart that they don't begin to interact prematurely. The ideal way to create a critical mass is to apply symmetrical pressure to one or more chunks of sub-critical material.

Compression: Greater density in the fissionable material gives the neutrons an optimized target-rich environment. The ideal method is an almost instantaneous symmetrical explosive force increasing the material's density to the required level for fission chain reaction.

Containment: Explosive fission is a race between the chain reaction's building power vs. a containment force holding things together long enough for the power to be really impressive when it does eventually blow. If the power overwhelms the containment too soon, it's a fizzle (low or no yield). The containment cannot be a function of any kind of ordinary material casing, a steel shell or anything like that. Those materials would be tissue paper against the (supposed) cumulative power of an explosive chain reaction in fissile material. The containment must come from a countervailing shock wave which very briefly – but strongly - constrains the building fission energy. The issue is that at the moment of assembly, the initiator releases a big spray of neutrons, so that early generation neutrons are bypassed. These plentiful neutrons act to build forces sufficient to overwhelm the containment, yet falling far short of the blast you really wanted.

When it starts off, if you have a lot of neutrons to start, you can't keep it together very long. It becomes vapor.

(Phillip Morrison)

But you have to try. The ideal form of containment is the symmetrical shock wave of implosion. Thus, we've piled up a bunch of motivations for implosion. Implosion was used in the Fat Man plutonium bomb to *create* the critical assembly, to *shrink* the plutonium sphere to enable supercriticality, and to *contain* the early reaction. This implosion was done by surrounding the plutonium and its outer material layers with precisely crafted explosives that were wired to detonate simultaneously, thus increasing the density while retaining a uniformly spherical (even while shrinking) geometry in the fissile mass, like quickly squashing a softball to golf ball size. Many thousands of pages have extolled the exquisite engineering of Fat Man's implosion mechanism. But let's consider the why and wherefore of it from 30,000 feet up, and see if backtracking through our implosion motivations list sheds any light.

It may seem obvious that squashing something will in some vaguely intuitive way build up energy or pressure that must be explosively released. In this case it's a specific increase in density which improves the fission cross-section (likelihood of productive neutron collisions). But a solid can only be compressed so much. And not so very much, because most of the 'space' in a solid is *within* its atoms, not *between* them. That's the whole idea of a solid. The atoms are already pretty much cheek by jowl (although allotrope geometries can be played with) but that little nucleus is still a 'mosquito in Memorial Stadium' from the incoming neutron's point of view.

A distinction is normally made between states in a fissile material: *subcritical*, *critical*, and *supercritical*. It's roughly analogous to animal populations, which may be declining, stable, or increasing. When fission events are not occurring, or are occurring only occasionally or with decreasing frequency, the mass is said to be *subcritical*. When fission events are occurring at a steady, linear pace that produces 'effective' (fission-causing) daughter neutrons at replacement rate (pay it forward), the reaction is *critical*: self-sustaining at a certain constant level of fissioning and heat generation. If the material can be kept cool enough, this can continue as long as fissionable fuel remains. If so many effective neutrons are produced at each generation that the rate of fissioning turns exponential, the material is said to be *supercritical*. If such a chain reaction, and the energies it produces, can be contained to provide for buildup over a sufficient (brief) time, it supposedly will explode.

But the boundary lines between these states are not carved in stone by God. The conditions they denote are probabilistic. In particular the 'line' between critical and supercritical is a broad spectrum of possible activity and outcomes, spanning a vast numerical and probabilistic landscape. However, none of those states is *explosive* - no matter what kind of enrichment, geometry, assembly, compression, initiation, containment or reflection may be attempted.

Furthermore, we know that implosive assembly is not required for supercriticality. We know that from the following sad history:

> *The demon core was a 6.2-kilogram (14 lb), 89-millimetre-diameter (3.5 in) subcritical mass of plutonium that was involved in two criticality accidents. It briefly went supercritical in two separate accidents at the Los Alamos laboratory in 1945 and 1946, and resulted in the acute radiation poisoning and subsequent deaths of scientists Harry Daghlian and Louis Slotin. After these incidents the spherical plutonium core was referred to as the "demon core".*
>
> (Wikipedia)

Slotin liked to work with the core halves by hand, using only a screwdriver to keep one piece just barely away from the other. One day his hand slipped, and one piece dropped onto the other, releasing a lethal radioactive particle spray. This shows that implosion is not needed for supercriticality. Two core hemispheres merely placed one atop the other go lethally critical immediately. The (conventionally accepted) reason that there was no blast is that containment was lacking.

A re-creation of the 1946 experiment. The beryllium hemisphere containing the plutonium core is held up with a screwdriver, which slipped, placing the plutonium hemispheres in critical assembly.

Some will scoff that there's no mystery about the need for implosion. Implosion is obviously needed for the following reason:

> The key idea in implosion assembly is to compress a subcritical spherical, or sometimes cylindrical, fissionable mass by using specially designed high explosives. Implosion works by initiating the detonation of the explosives on their outer surface, so that the detonation wave moves inward. Careful design allows the creation of a smooth, symmetrical implosion shock wave. This shock wave is transmitted to the fissionable core and compresses it, raising the density to the point of supercriticality.

(nuclearweaponarchive.org)

But we've just seen that *density* and *critical assembly* can't be the main motivation for implosion. Now let's talk about *containment*. So far we've focused on Fat Man, the plutonium implosion bomb. In the case of Little Boy, critical assembly was not achieved with implosive compression, but by rapid forced proximity. A hollow uranium cylinder was fired along the barrel of a sort of cannon, to force fit it around a uranium spike at the far end of the 'gun'.

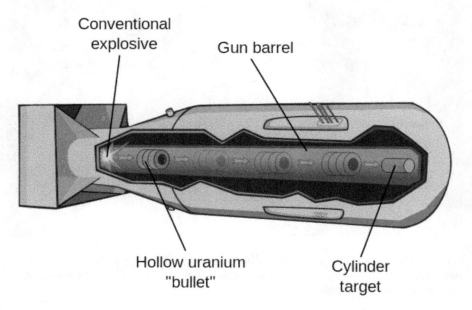

'Gun' type nuclear weapon (Little Boy) Adopting the Coster-Mullen configuration of hollow rings as the projectile 'bullet'. Full attribution and credits for this illustration are in 'Bibliography' section.

It seems the implosion is crucially required to serve as a very short-term containment for the forces building in the first instants of criticality. If the energies and temperatures pressing outward are too intense too early the device will be destroyed, dispersing the contiguity of atoms needed to propagate the chain reaction, and resulting in low or little blast yield. You want a few additional generations of fission before things melt or fly apart – 'become vapor'. Implosion, with its intense symmetrical incoming shock wave, seems to fit the bill.

But here's the problem: there was no such 'containment' requirement for the 'gun' critical assembly used in Little Boy. That's obvious, because the explosive adjacency created there was not symmetric. The design thus left at least some unreinforced, or unequally reinforced, dimensions effectively open as an escape route for energies generated early in the process. This, very broadly speaking, is why Little Boy could not have worked. It would become 'vapor' (if a chain reaction had been initiated at all, which is doubtful).

The science here is radically different from the situation with fusion, yet a crude illustrative analogy can be made between the problem with the 'gun' design and the fatal flaw which doomed Edward Teller's initial vision for the classical 'Super' hydrogen bomb, which was to be triggered by a fission explosion at one end of a tube of fusion fuel. Los Alamos physicist Richard Garwin stated: *"You can't get cylindrical containers of deuterium to burn because the energy escapes faster than it reproduces itself."* The energy is not properly contained to the cylinder.

Nevertheless, according to conventional thought at the time, a 'gun' assembly (where there is no implosive, symmetric compression) ought to work just fine, not only with uranium, but with plutonium also. In fact, a gun assembly plutonium bomb, 'Thin Man', was attempted and abandoned in mid-stream. Instead they switched over to implosion – but for the plutonium bomb only. Officially that switchover was not motivated by any of the considerations cited above.

Gun style assembly was deemed infeasible because the most available plutonium at Los Alamos was pile-produced Pu239 - with the Pu240 isotope inextricably mixed in. Skipping over a lot of complications, plutonium contaminated with Pu240 is overly sensitive to free neutrons that may be present in or near the sub-critical mass. Free neutrons are those that occur in the natural background or from spontaneous fission. If a 'background neutron' got its nose under the wire, into the fissile mass, it could trigger supercriticality leading to pre-detonation. That could happen in the fractional time window as the projectile piece approaches the target piece inside the gun barrel, at the very moment of bomb detonation. For weapons purposes, pre-detonation really isn't 'detonation' at all. It means a dud bomb that burns itself out before you have a chance to blow anything up properly. A fizzle.

Therefore, implosion is supposedly required to create criticality nearly instantaneously, triggering the fullest possible fissioning at a time strictly of your own choosing. You have to go critical fast enough to beat out any loose neutrons.

> *It was apparent that the gun assembly would not give a high enough velocity to beat the neutron background. The laboratory was reorganized in August 1944 to apply major effort to developing an alternative method of assembling a mass of plutonium, the implosion method.*
>
> ('The Los Alamos Primer' Robert Serber)

The cover story runs that pile produced plutonium's greater reactivity (as opposed to U235) forced this design change. But in fact the gun design was unworkable for *any choice of material*. Because there is no combination of timings and assembly forces that would prevent the thing from melting into slag at detonation. If the neutron background was a concern for the plutonium gun, it should have been a concern for the uranium gun as well.

> [It was known to the Project scientists that] *cosmic rays, which were more numerous at Los Alamos, owing to the laboratory's high altitude (up to 7,000 feet), were inducing fission in their U235 samples, an effect showing up as false spontaneous fission counts.*
>
> ('Critical Assembly' Hoddeson et al.)

Neutrons come from outer space:

> *The Earth and all living things on it are constantly bombarded by radiation from outer space. This radiation primarily consists of positively charged ions derived from sources outside our solar system. This radiation interacts with atoms in the atmosphere to create an air shower of secondary radiation, including X-rays, muons, protons, alpha particles, pions, electrons, and neutrons. The immediate dose from cosmic radiation is largely from muons, neutrons, and electrons, and this dose varies in different parts of the world based largely on the altitude. For example, the city of Denver in the United States (at 1650 meters elevation) receives a cosmic ray dose roughly twice that of a location at sea level. This radiation is much more intense in the upper troposphere, around 10 km altitude [32,808 feet], and is thus of particular concern for airline crews.* (Wikipedia)

Now consider that the gun design was to be a bomb, transported and delivered by airplane at altitudes up to 30,000 feet or greater. The separation of sub-critical material within the device was dictated, not by the need to forestall interaction with background neutrons, but simply by the dimensions of the B-29 bomb bay.

In Little Boy, several feet in the gun barrel separated the critical masses, and the device was fuzed to detonate at around 2,000 feet. You may think pre-detonation is strictly a matter of micro- or nano-distances and imperceptible timescales at the very moment of assembly, just as 'seating' of the masses against or into one another is occurring. Thus, it wouldn't be a concern at macro (visible and tangible) scales? Not so. (Keep in mind that 'pre-detonation' is, in a sense, not 'detonation' at all but a fizzle pop or complete dud). Consider this fact about uranium transport:

> As [uranium] oxide or metal the material travels in small cans that are placed in a cylinder – a five inch pipe – that is braced with welded struts in the center of an ordinary fifty-five-gallon steel drum. It is for criticality reasons that the uranium is held in the center with the airspace of the drum around it, for if too much U235, in any form, were to come too close together it would go critical, start to fission, and irradiate the surrounding countryside.

('The Curve of Binding Energy' John McPhee)

If the 'gun' designers, even for U235, had been serious, they would have had to consider transport and handling of the device against the neutron background at high altitude.

Backing up a little, the "implosion" crisis during the spring of 1944 is usually represented as a combination of:

1. abandonment of the 'gun' assembly method for the plutonium bomb, due to the plutonium isotope mixture problems cited above.

2. consequent shift of emphasis to the super-innovative and vastly more sophisticated implosion design.

You may wonder why they didn't apply as much effort to separating out the PU240 isotope from the PUS239 (and thus supposedly rescuing the 'gun' design for plutonium) as they ended up devoting to perfecting the implosion process. Good question. Under the circumstances, that would have been the correct call. They already knew about non-chemical purification methods (the chemical impurities problem had already been solved for plutonium by this time), as that would have been analogous to the U235 separation challenge. The same degree of fast-turnaround genius innovation could as well have been applied to that problem as to the super-subtle and difficult implosion thing. But they didn't go down that road, mainly because *nothing* would have saved the 'gun' design. As an attendee at the July 17 1944 meeting recalled in his notes:

> *The choice was to junk the whole discovery of the chain reaction that produced plutonium, and all of the investment in time and effort of the Hanford plant, unless somebody could come up with a way of assembling the plutonium into a weapon that would explode.*
> ('Critical Assembly' Hoddeson et al.)

He's basically admitting that the insistence on continuing with a plutonium weapon, though they had a 'perfectly working' uranium gun weapon almost ready to go, was a PR decision, not a military one. Remember that the military objective was simply '*a bomb that would explode*'. It was supposedly in the bag, and all effort should have been devoted to fuel stockpiling and bomb manufacture at that point.

But there must have been another realization at that same time, (we can call it the 'gun crisis'). Not only was the 'gun' design abandoned for plutonium in favor of implosion, but *the 'gun' design was abandoned for the uranium bomb also*. Oppenheimer summarized the cover story in his July 18 1944 report to Groves as follows:

> *In the light of the above facts, it appears reasonable to discontinue the intensive effort to achieve higher purity for plutonium and to concentrate attention on methods of assembly which do not require a low neutron background for their success. At the present time the method to which an overriding priority must be assigned is the method of implosion.*
>
> ('Critical Assembly' Hoddeson et al.)

I believe it had become tacitly understood that the uranium gun design was unworkable. What to do? Openly admit that this path was a dead-end, while continuing to sincerely pursue the implosion? That would be problematic for the following reasons:

1. The cost and effort involved in producing the enriched uranium fuel for the uranium bomb. Other uses could have been found for that uranium, but it would have been felt as a major failure.
2. The future 'success' of the implosion option itself was far from guaranteed at the time. If the 'Thin Man' gun concept was admitted infeasible (for reasons quite apart from fuel type or quality) and openly abandoned, and if the implosion option also fizzled, it might then be too late or too difficult to fake *anything*, to get any kind of result for the Manhattan Project as a whole.

Better to hedge bets by continued tweaking of a 'gun' design bomb as a parallel show operation – known as Little Boy. Which, after all, did turn out to have a kind of military utility in its own right. Just as a false pill (placebo) can cure real disease, it may have been reasonably conjectured that a fake bomb, supported with proper staging and props, could help end the war on the United States terms. *Trickery is the way of war.*

As the final nail in the coffin of the 'gun design' scam (both plutonium Thin Man and uranium Little Boy), let's consider how Edward Teller's infamous 'Super' mania (prospect of a hydrogen bomb of arbitrary, even world-ending, yield) was treated during the war years at Los Alamos. It's worth going through a few quotes to establish the general thinking on it before I make the key point tying this to the 'implosion crisis'.

For Bethe, Serber, and Oppenheimer, the Super was at best an interesting possibility - one worthy of further study, but only after the atomic bomb was already in hand.

('Brotherhood of the Bomb' Gregg Herken)

Oppenheimer said that he now believed the superbomb would require a minimum of three more years to reach production.

('Brotherhood of the Bomb' Gregg Herken)

Enthusiasm for the Super was probably highest in the fall of 1942, when ... the difficulties with Super operation were not yet obvious.

('Critical Assembly' Hoddeson et al.)

Oppenheimer stated: "This possibility has been considered in detail and it is highly probable that in principle the scheme is feasible. It will need more development than the gadget. But arrangements should be made that its development follow immediately the completion of the gadget." Thus, while the Super was being discussed by the scientists at the laboratory, it was already clear that the project was of secondary importance.

('Critical Assembly' Hoddeson et al.)

By February 1944, it was clear that making a Super would be far more difficult than originally thought, and research on the thermonuclear weapon began to receive less attention. Only Teller's theoretical group and Egon Bretscher's small experimental group that measured cross-sections relevant to the Super continued to work on the problem. ... In September 1943, Teller felt optimistic enough to ask the Governing Board to increase the level of the Super effort. As further justification, Teller cited indications that the Germans were going to use deuterium for similar purposes. However, the Governing Board recommended that no more than one full-time person should work on the problem.

> In February 1944, [Konopinski] suggested increasing the priority of the program. But the board did not wish to expand Super work, because "the members of the board desired to produce something that would play a part in this war."
>
> ('Critical Assembly' Hoddeson et al.)

So here in the Super proposal, we have a perfect contrast to how the implosion proposal was treated. The 'Super' thing was quite correctly judged to be too complex, too uncertain, likely to be too resource-hungry and just not a fit to the rigorous purpose of the Los Alamos lab. As stated at the outset by Serber himself, the purpose was to make a working bomb for immediate military application. It was to significantly affect, perhaps win, the present war. It was wartime! So they did the right thing to relegate the Super to the bench. Now, what about the gun gadget and the implosion weapon?

> *The gun gadget offered a sense of security to the laboratory because of its perceived simplicity. Devoid of the technical complexities of implosion, the gun offered scientists an excellent chance to develop an atomic bomb in time to help with the war effort and fulfill the laboratory's mission to build a bomb.*
>
> ('Critical Assembly' Hoddeson et al.)

So they *had* a weapon that according to the cover story, was *guaranteed* (if you quibble with the strength of that assertion you are undercutting the whole orthodox explanation, repeated in every reference source, of why the gun device was not tested). It had every imaginable military advantage and could even be readily converted to an artillery shell. With a full complement of these, the United States could have leveled Germany, Japan, *and* the Soviet Union and become the last man standing. Which the USA kind of became anyway – but remember we're talking about wartime here, the thick of combat, when outcomes were not at all certain. The only certainty was: *the gun bomb is guaranteed to work*. It will obliterate a city or any other target site – vaporize the enemy and all his works off the face of the earth.

On that basis, the only correct, logical and sane military choice would have been to put the implosion device aside for the duration, and concentrate every dollar, every man-hour, every ounce of material, every square foot of lab space to the 'gun' bomb. Build a stockpile – now! There would have been nothing else in the military mind, certainly not in Leslie Groves' mind. If you say uranium was still scarce, I'll agree, but so was plutonium at that point. The same bulked-load of genius that was devoted to getting symmetrical implosion to work would have been entirely devoted to uranium enrichment. If those weren't the right people for that new emphasis, Groves should have fired them and gotten hundreds of new scientists who *were* right for it. The gun design's perfect utility left only one challenge, a 'known' challenge, a problem with well understood dimensions – uranium enrichment.

Or, if they really had such a mania for pure research, knowing the gun design was perfected in every other way, they could also have worked on separating out the PU240 isotope from the pile-produced plutonium, as required to keep Thin Man viable. That (non-chemical) purification would have been challenging, but not necessarily (given the limited knowledge they had at the time of the 'implosion crisis') much more so than getting implosion to work at all.

The only logical conclusion is that the gun design was seen to be a failure no matter how it was tweaked, no matter what fuel they used. They had to desperately double down, hoping against hope that the implosion would turn out to be their ace in the hole. Otherwise, rather than making the speculative implosion weapon the focus of everything, they would have treated it as they did the Super – a longer-term, not-for-this-war research possibility. Of course, by the FAIL hypothesis, the implosion method ended up failing too, but they did commit to a sincere effort on it. If the 'gun' had been functional as advertised, they would have started frantically piling up a huge inventory of 'gun' bombs, to win the war and rule the world.

From that time forward, the 'gun' project carried on as a mixture of basic research and operational scam – but not as a working weapons program. Activity certainly continued though. After all, a lot of the same elements would be needed for a fake show - documentation, diagnostic equipment and experiments, dimensional analysis, support materials and tools, special laboratories and project teams, etc. - as for a real one.

The Secret

Let's back up for a moment and ponder the eternal question of *will* vs. *reality*. If a military rationale can be developed for the hydrogen bomb (as currently conceived) then it's not too great a stretch to assume somebody could cook up an equally legitimate military purpose for a Doomsday weapon. Such a rationale was humorously described in Stanley Kubrick's brilliant nuke movie 'Dr. Strangelove':

> *When you merely wish to bury bombs, there is no limit to the size. After that they are connected to a gigantic complex of computers. A specific and clearly defined set of circumstances, under which the bombs are to be exploded, is programmed into a tape memory bank. If you take, say, fifty H-bombs in the hundred megaton range and jacket them with cobalt thorium G, when they are exploded they will produce a doomsday shroud. Cobalt thorium G has a radioactive half-life of ninety three years. When it is detonated, it will produce enough lethal radioactive fallout so that lethal cloud of radioactivity will encircle the earth for ninety three years! Within ten months, the surface of the earth will be as dead as the moon! The doomsday machine is designed to trigger itself automatically. It is designed to explode if any attempt is ever made to untrigger it. There are those of us who fought against it, but in the end we could not keep up with the expense involved in the arms race, the space race, and the peace race. Our doomsday scheme cost us just a small fraction of what we'd been spending on defense in a single year. But the deciding factor was when we learned that your country was working along similar lines, and we were afraid of a doomsday gap.*
>
> ('Dr. Strangelove')

The above comic logic isn't so different from the serious military thinking that goes into strategic defense and attack planning. So let's take another look at *igniting the atmosphere* in the light of the fictional example above. Ignition of the atmosphere was a question that came up early in the Manhattan Project, mentioned in an earlier chapter ('Burn the Sky'; BTS hereafter). One could easily imagine a sort of Manhattan Project that would have as its goal development of precisely that: a BTS Doomsday Machine that would ignite the entire atmosphere. As we saw earlier, this was brought up as a danger in the early stages of the Manhattan Project.

In these discussions, the bomb that might have had the side-effect of igniting the entire atmosphere of the earth is referred to as the 'Super' – a hypothetical true hydrogen bomb, as later (supposedly) developed for real by Edward Teller.

> *Horrific as the theoretical Super might be, there was still another, even grimmer specter that haunted the theorists: the possibility that an exploding superbomb might release enough energy to ignite the nitrogen in the atmosphere, incinerating the planet. Bethe dismissed that possibility instinctively and later claimed to have disproved it with a few quick calculations.*
>
> *Bethe discovered that Teller's earlier calculations had underestimated the effects of a fundamental process in physics – the manner in which the energy of a nuclear explosion is dissipated through radiation. Not only did radiative cooling keep the planet safe from incineration by hydrogen bombs, Bethe pointed out, but it probably made the hypothetical Super itself unworkable. Konopinski briefly rescued Teller's thesis by proposing to light the deuterium with tritium, which has a lower ignition temperature. But Bethe seemingly knocked that theory flat, too.*

('Brotherhood of the Bomb' Gregg Herken)

Hans Bethe was a genius physicist and Nobel laureate (1967, stellar nucleosynthesis). He played a key role in all the original work on the fission bomb and the later 'hydrogen' bomb. I'm not citing him as an explicit ally in the quest to explode the nuclear hoax. But this true nuclear side-story makes a very deep and relevant point. This BTS history is a great illustration that some things simply don't work, aren't possible given the physical constraints of reality. Why has no BTS machine been developed? Don't tell me our leaders are too sane and humane and sensible for it. We're way beyond that kindergarten stuff at this point. The reason it's not done is solely because *it isn't possible*.

We latter-day analysts may not be geniuses on the order of Hans Bethe. But notice how he did the job: *'put in the numbers'*, *'a few quick calculations'*... that kind of thing. Basically, he was one guy and a slide rule. And that's all he needed to *'knock that theory flat'*. As we've seen in the earlier chapter, the computing capabilities of the full Manhattan Project were not much better:

> Bethe acknowledged receipt of the IBM machines on 4 April, mentioning that the machines had been put to use in implosion calculations. To check the program, Metropolis and Feynman made parallel calculations using hand-operated Marchant machines, staffed by a group of women who were part of the work force of the laboratory. Like the components of a computer, each carried out a particular step. Feynman later explained: "We worked out all the numerical steps that the machines were supposed to do - multiply this, and then do this, and subtract that." He recalled, "[This woman] *was the multiplier, and* [that woman] *was the adder, and this one cubed, and we had index cards, and all she did was cube this number and send it to the next one. We went through our cycle this way until we got all the bugs out."* The human computer actually developed speed - the same as that predicted for the IBM machines. But as Feynman noted, "the IBM machines didn't get tired and could work three shifts. The girls got tired after a while."
>
> ('Critical Assembly' Hoddeson et al.)

Think of it: a computer working at the 'same speed' as *a bunch of people passing index cards around*. Yet that machine, supplemented by individual slide rules, was sufficient for the numerical work on the bomb's theory, design and engineering. Just to take one example of how almost incalculably far beyond those Stone Age simulation tools (early IBM machines or human calculators) anybody with a MacBook or PC is today, consider Monte Carlo probabilistic sampling methods, which were:

> ... *central to the simulations required for the Manhattan Project, though severely limited by the computational tools at the time.*
>
> (Wikipedia)

Monte Carlo statistical sampling methods were pioneered at Los Alamos by Stanislaw Ulam:

> *The first thoughts and attempts I made to practice* [the Monte Carlo Method] *were suggested by a question which occurred to me in 1946 as I was convalescing from an illness and playing solitaires. The question was what are the chances that a Canfield solitaire laid out with 52 cards will come out successfully? After spending a lot of time trying to estimate them by pure combinatorial calculations, I wondered whether a more practical method than "abstract thinking" might not be to lay it out say one hundred times and simply observe and count the number of successful plays. This was already possible to envisage with the beginning of the new era of fast computers, and I immediately thought of problems of neutron diffusion and other questions of mathematical physics, and more generally how to change processes described by certain differential equations into an equivalent form interpretable as a succession of random operations. Later* [in 1946], *I described the idea to John von Neumann, and we began to plan actual calculations.*
>
> ('Stan Ulam, John Von Neumann, and the Monte Carlo Method' Roger Eckhardt)

Von Neumann described application of these methods to problems in neutron diffusion, specified the parametric model, and estimated the computational cost:

> *I append a tentative "computing sheet" for the calculation shown. It should give a reasonably immediate idea of the amount of work that is involved in the procedure in question.*

> *I cannot assert this with certainty yet, but it seems to me that the instructions given on this "computing sheet" do not exceed the logical capacity of the ENIAC. I doubt that the processing of 100 'neutrons' will take much longer than the reading, punching and (once) sorting time of 100 cards; i.e. about 3 minutes. Hence taking 100 of these 'neutrons' through 100 of these stages should take about 300 minutes, i.e., 5 hours.*
>
> ('Stan Ulam, John Von Neumann, and the Monte Carlo Method' Roger Eckhardt)

Geological time by current standards. And that was running a severely simplified model:

> *In his formulation von Neumann used a spherically symmetric geometry in which the various materials of interest varied only with the radius. He assumed that the neutrons were generated isotropically and had a known velocity spectrum and that the absorption, scattering, and fission cross-sections in the fissionable material and any surrounding materials (such as neutron moderators or reflectors) could be described as a function of neutron velocity. The idea then was to trace out the history of a given neutron, using random digits to select the outcomes of the various interactions along the way.*
>
> ('Stan Ulam, John Von Neumann, and the Monte Carlo Method' Roger Eckhardt)

Note that a usable simulation must not only incorporate realistic upgrades to all the drastic simplifications in Von Neumann's neutron diffusion model, but it must incorporate factors that are completely missing there. For example, fission creates not only additional neutrons to maintain the chain reaction. It also creates *fission fragments*, lower-numbered elements that are the shards of the fissile material's atoms after successful encounters. These shards are then moving in the material with their own energy, which contributes to the buildup against which the containment force must work (to give the explosive fission adequate preparation time before it steps into the spotlight with a big flash-bang). The fission fragments are thus yet another hindrance in the containment's 'race against time', one that is rarely discussed or modeled adequately.

All that is just one part of one process, merely an example of the demands made by a truly adequate simulation. With current cloud-based statistical and machine learning frameworks, these kinds of simulations become trivial. We can even integrate much more sophisticated versions of Monte Carlo and other statistical methods, for example the use of mean field genetic-type sampling for estimating particle transmission energies, and heuristic natural search algorithms in evolutionary computing.

Any average Joe now has access to a MacBook or PC with millions of times the hardware computing and storage power of the entire Manhattan Project, its affiliated university-based orbital groups, and all its industrial partners of the time put together. Those resources are matched or exceeded by the software modeling facilities available that, essentially for free, give you access to analytical power vastly exceeding all the number-crunching physicists in the Manhattan Project. These incomparably superior basic resources, combined with over seven decades of accumulated public knowledge put the amateur modeler light-years ahead of the Manhattan Project at its peak. And if Bethe could rule out 'burn the sky' in a few minutes of slide-ruling, a dedicated modeler can crack the secret of explosive fission using the resources listed above.

And there *is* a secret of explosive fission. That much is true. But it's way different than you might think. We've seen that there's no serious lack of nuclear materials. We've also seen that technical knowledge is openly available.

> *Half a century of official and unofficial dissemination of information from the nuclear weapons laboratories together with the normal publication processes in cognate branches of physics and engineering, mean that much of the relevant explicit knowledge is now irrevocably in the public domain.*
>
> ('Tacit Knowledge, Weapons Design, and the Uninvention of Nuclear Weapons' MacKenzie and Spinard)

More and more countries claim to be joining the Nuclear Club. But decade after decade, nothing gets openly nuked. *That's because it's not possible.* That's the secret of explosive fission. Pure FAIL right from the starting gun. But it's a secret I can only refer to, not fully reveal. The nuclear powers don't mind goofups in materials handling. They don't mind weapons design espionage and technical information leaks. As long as revelations and speculations serve to reinforce the FEAR, it's all good. But they'd come down hard as nails on somebody who convincingly refuted the entire proposition. Their instrument would be what we've already looked at: the Atomic Energy Act of 1946 – *born secret.*

In a previous chapter, we've examined the feasibility of a Virtual Manhattan Project. The reason I can assert the FAIL hypothesis so forcefully is that I have created my own full simulation of a nuclear device – actually one of each type (Little Boy, Fat Man). In doing this, I have relied strictly, solely and entirely on openly published source material, including the technical references used in the preparation of this book (see Bibliography) and other open source or public domain information not listed in this book.

Publicly accessible simulations of partial aspects of fission have been created before. But they are toys, because they accept the reality of explosive fission and devote the modeling effort mainly to providing a visually appealing show to support the starting assumption. The few knobs they provide for user control (how many fissile atoms, degrees of compression, neutron diffusion coefficients, etc.) all stem entirely from the initial unquestioning acceptance of the FEAR assumption. They *assume* what they set out to *prove.*

Current public software simulations and demonstrations of fission are toys, much along the lines of the earlier efforts at Berkeley and the first phase of the Manhattan Project.

> *Most of the theorists lent a hand in the difficult and crucial task of modeling neutron diffusion, which was important to both critical mass and efficiency calculations. This effort had begun as Berkeley before the start of Project Y, with the extrapolated end-point method, for modeling the movement of neutrons in the bomb. But the assumptions were too simplified for anything other than a rudimentary model: all*

> neutrons had the same velocity, the tamper and core were stationary, every neutron collision was elastic, neutrons were scattered isotropically, and neutrons in the core and tamper had the same mean free path.
>
> ('Critical Assembly Hoddeson et al.)

My simulations, in contrast, include realistic factors like those outlined below, which Bethe supposedly insisted on. We've already seen that things like these were omitted in Von Neumann's proposed modeling on ENIAC for the post-war period. Clearly the wartime Manhattan Project did not have the computational resources to implement these kinds of features:

> In October 1943, Bethe assigned top priority to finding a more realistic description of neutron diffusion through the core of the bomb. That meant taking into account the fact that the neutrons had a distribution of velocities, that the neutrons did not scatter isotropically, and that mean free paths were different in the tamper and the core.
>
> ('Critical Assembly Hoddeson et al.)

My simulation starts *ab initio* – not from the endpoint of FEAR (or FAIL either for that matter) but from the theory known to the Manhattan scientists and the final design components of their device – but minus the assumption that it has to work. Unlike other simulations, I require the *bang* as output, not input.

My model is generous, in that I do not apply constraints based on incidentals of military application. Half of the admittedly brilliant reverse-engineering work by Coster-Mullen is devoted to conformity with military constraints of the time, and synchrony with mission-specific delivery processes used by the 509th. My simulation is not constrained by deliverability in a B-29 or any other vehicle. My only constraints relate to fissionability with historically specified fuels and materials. The hard constraints I impose are the commonly accepted boundaries and properties of 20th century, white bread, mainstream physics only. Otherwise, I incorporate ranges of values that would allow the model to function in any way that could conceivably fit reality so defined.

In crafting my software simulation, I have had the advantage of theoretical, engineering, and analytic modeling tools far exceeding what the actual Manhattan Project had in their projections, estimates, and component testing. The result of my simulation is this: **Explosive nuclear fission is not possible. Nuclear weapons are a hoax. The FEAR proposition is false.**

Because of the 'born secret' thing, I cannot share the code or the quantitative summary of the principle that invalidates the FEAR hypothesis. My own work is *born secret*, self-classified from its creation, legally speaking hidden from my own eyes. I can't take the chance or afford the hassle of being extradited by the United States and charged (or more likely, held indefinitely without charge). That's why this book emphasizes all the other, *circumstantial evidence* against FEAR. I do understand that's it's frustrating not to have access to the full numerical and process proof of the FAIL proposition.

The implosion bomb itself is a fitting metaphor for the situation. A sphere of nuclear fissionable material, the bomb's core, sits at the center, entirely surrounded by high explosive charges (which are used to compress it to super-criticality). If you detonated the high explosives but didn't get the energy buildup from the chain reaction in the required narrow time window, the result would be a nasty bang by normal standards. But it wouldn't approach the expected total nuclear annihilation and vaporization.

By analogy, because information relating to the design of nuclear weapons is automatically born classified, I cannot hand you the 'core' – the shocking model code which reveals the falsity of explosive fission. But I can at least detonate all the surrounding stuff – that is, I can present the reams of circumstantial evidence against the FEAR hypothesis. That has been my goal with this book.

This book could therefore be seen as only the Introduction to a complete listing of the refutation simulation. I understand that readers would prefer to see the real plutonium-fueled mushroom cloud - the final bulletproof quantitative refutation. Just as we'd like to see Bethe's original calculations for contradicting the BTS scenario. I'm sorry not to provide the full model here. But use the highly explosive circumstantial evidence that I *have* assembled to detonate your illusions about the FEAR proposition.

'Implosive charges surrounding core' as rhetorical metaphor. This book's voluminous circumstantial evidence is analogous to the high explosives (white-faced chunks) packed around the outer circumference of the central core, which represents the full numeric simulation.

Money Shot: TRINITY

It works!

First words of J. Robert Oppenheimer on viewing the
Trinity test explosion

After the war was over, Admiral Nimitz visited our laboratory. We described what we did and that the explosion was equal to 20,000 tons of dynamite. He said "You might believe it, but I don't" and he walked out.

Morton Camac ('Atom Bombs' John Coster-Mullen)

The first test of a fully assembled nuclear bomb was the imploded plutonium Gadget, supposedly detonated near Alamogordo, New Mexico.

Trinity was the code name of the first detonation of a nuclear weapon. It was conducted by the United States Army at 5:29 am on July 16, 1945, as part of the Manhattan Project. The test was conducted in the Jornada del Muerto desert about 35 miles (56 km) southeast of Socorro, New Mexico, on what was then the USAAF Alamogordo Bombing and Gunnery Range (now part of White Sands Missile Range). The only structures originally in the vicinity were the McDonald Ranch House and its ancillary buildings, which scientists used as a laboratory for testing bomb components. A base camp was constructed, and there were 425 people present on the weekend of the test.

(Wikipedia)

For the FAIL idea to fly, the Trinity test must have been faked. It's often said that extraordinary claims require extraordinary evidence. The existence of explosive fission, the FEAR hypothesis, is certainly an extraordinary claim. But nobody could deny that the Trinity test is the most intensely convincing event story ever offered as proof of anything.

Yes, of all the stories supporting the FEAR hypothesis, the TRINITY test saga and apparent result is the hardest for nuclear weapons skeptics to handle. When you see photographs of the explosion, and its aftermath, and then read the testimonials of the many witnesses on the ground and the observers in the air, and read about various nuclear innocents who noticed unusual effects from far distances, it seems inconceivable that any staging or fakery was involved. It is with the Trinity test that a fair-minded reader would be most justified in closing the books on the FEAR hypothesis - in its favor. But I have to play the ball where it lies. I'm committed to raking through the embers, looking for anything suspicious - so let's get to it.

Something Like an Actor

Theoretical physicist J. Robert Oppenheimer was the founding director of the Los Alamos lab portion of the Manhattan Project, and is often called the father of the atomic bomb. Interestingly, Oppenheimer once slipped by opining, in late May 1945, that *"the atomic bomb is shit"*. Historians naturally assume that he was trying to say that it would be far too powerful to apply to any practical, precise and proper military objective. Still, it's an odd remark. More than sixty-five German and Japanese cities had been blasted and roasted to rubble by then. That was seen in the context of the times as highly effective war-fighting – otherwise it wouldn't have continued. The atomic bomb would achieve with one plane in a few minutes the effect of hundreds of planes loaded to the gills sweeping back and forth for hours, exposed to all kinds of hazards. How could atomic supplementation not be perceived as a militarily useful upgrade?

If you think that Oppenheimer was perhaps basing his crudely stated assessment (above) on an inflated idea of the bomb's likely power (for example, he maybe thought it would have made all of Honshu uninhabitable for a thousand years), think again. In the immediately pre-Trinity betting pool held by the scientists, Oppenheimer gambled on a yield number: 300 tons of TNT. Not kilotons. Tons. A tiny fraction of the 20 or so kilotons that (by report) actually resulted. So it can't be that he feared it as a superweapon.

The man had devoted years of his life and his entire professional reputation to the project. How could he say it was '*shit*'? How could he doubt its military value? If he thought superweapons were shit, why sign on to the project in the first place? Or, if he really believed it was a superweapon that could never be used, surely a brain of his stature would grasp that, even if never used, such an object would be of huge military value in the larger strategic sense of intimidation, deterrence, etc. If it were never used, so much the better. But we have it direct from arguably the greatest military mind of all time:

> 是故百戰百勝，非善之善也；不戰而屈人之兵，善之善者也。
>
> *Thus, to fight and win a hundred battles is not the ultimate greatness; the ultimate greatness is to beat down the enemy without ever fighting at all.*
>
> 故兵貴勝，不貴久。
>
> *In war let your object be victory, not lengthy campaigns.*
>
> ('The Art of War' Sunzi)

Is that not a likely result of the bomb, if it could be shown working to spec? And is not this kind of bloodless capitulation a 'military' benefit? The book is called '*The Art of War*' after all. Oppenheimer, with his vaunted philosophical sensitivity would have been alive to this 'military' wisdom – *if he thought it applied*. By May 1945, for some reason, the prospects were looking dim to him. Why? The theory said everything had to work perfectly. And yet '*the atom bomb is shit*'.

Maybe it was merely a slip of the tongue. Or - a slip of the mask? Prize-winning chronicler of the nuclear age Richard Rhodes once opined in a filmed interview:

> *Oppenheimer was a fascinating and complicated man. Fundamentally he seemed to have had some of the qualities of an actor.*

Maybe that is a word to the wise, if we have ears to catch the hint.

Unit Testing?

To me, the most amazing thing about Trinity was that the Gadget exploded powerfully and perfectly the first time out. You may chide me and call my astonishment unwarranted. After all, surely they'd made hundreds if not thousands of successful component tests prior to blowing up the fully assembled final product. Let's think about that for a moment.

I'm very familiar with large-scale software development. In software, testing is a big thing. It's called SQA – Software Quality Assurance. Though software and hardware are not quite the same beast, all complex systems have some common features. For software, there are many levels and types of testing, but the main distinction for this discussion is between unit testing and integration testing.

Unit testing is described as follows:

> *Unit testing refers to tests that verify the functionality of a specific section of code, usually at the function level. These types of tests are usually written by developers as they work on code to ensure that the specific function is working as expected. Unit testing alone cannot verify the functionality of a piece of software, but rather is used to ensure that the building blocks of the software work independently from each other. Unit testing is a software development process that involves synchronized application of a broad spectrum of defect prevention and detection strategies in order to reduce software development risks, time, and costs. It is performed by the software developer or engineer during the construction phase of the software development lifecycle. Unit testing aims to eliminate construction errors before code is promoted to QA; this strategy is intended to increase the quality of the resulting software as well as the efficiency of the overall development and QA process.* (Wikipedia)

Money Shot: TRINITY

So unit testing is component testing of pieces of the final system in isolation. A hardware system, especially one as complex as the Trinity Gadget, has lots of subsystems that can be checked in various ways prior to final integration. Some aspects of the implosive compression were ingeniously unit tested with radioactive lanthanum placed at the center of a (non plutonium) test sphere, such that recorded changes in gamma rays emitted through the course of the firing event could be correlated to effects. That's the kind of thing even I have to admire and call clever experimental science.

But, for another example, the high explosive shell surrounding the core had been 'unit tested' with blanks just days prior to Trinity – and it failed. The explosive 'lenses' were found not to have fired simultaneously, and they would not have compressed the core properly.

> *Instead of the nuclear core, instruments* [were] *placed inside the sphere to measure the force of the implosion. I hadn't yet heard the outcome of the test, or even if it had taken place. When I arrived at the Trinity test site I learned that it had failed! I wondered why we were still going ahead with a test of the whole gadget... I learned a bit later, the Trinity test was going ahead because Bethe had looked at the blank test data and shown that it was the instrumentation itself that had failed. Although the lenses might still have been defective, or improperly designed, the failed test was no proof that they were the problem.*
>
> ('Rider of the Pale Horse: A Memoir of Los Alamos and Beyond'
> McAllister H. Hull)

First of all, we can commend this example of hardware 'unit testing'. That's the way to go. But we can still be appalled by the finding that the test itself was (supposedly) the problem. This means that, in effect, no unit testing was done at all on this critical component. In the world of professional software engineering, no programmer would dare to 'check in' his piece without performing any unit tests. That would be a recipe for disaster.

In a good outfit, there is a full 'build' every night and automated checks of the whole system, known as *integration tests*, are run.

> *Integration testing is any type of software testing that seeks to verify the interfaces between components against a software design. Software components may be integrated in an iterative way or all together ("big bang"). Normally the former is considered a better practice since it allows interface issues to be located more quickly and fixed. Integration testing works to expose defects in the interfaces and interaction between integrated components (modules). Progressively larger groups of tested software components corresponding to elements of the architectural design are integrated and tested until the software works as a system.*
>
> (Wikipedia)

Any unverified component must be considered broken. If the failed module was yours, you arrive early the next morning to find that you *broke the build*. This is a terrible hit to your reputation and, what's worse, you have to buy pizza for the whole team.

> *It was really unnerving when the blank shot failed. The normal anxiety that one might have had with a device which you had worked on but which had never been tested was heightened by the failure of the blank shot.*
>
> (McAllister Hull Manhattan Project Technician)

The Gadget was complex, make up of many subcomponents. We stand in awe of a 'build' that worked with effectively no unit testing and only one integration run (Trinity shot). This is unheard of even in fairly modest software systems. In engineering it would be like building a bridge with steel that had never undergone at least sample testing of load deflection and strength. Oh well. It was wartime. And maybe applied nuclear physics, by the standards of 1945, was a more tractable and forgiving field than software engineering has turned out to be.

Jumbo

The story of Jumbo is another interesting Trinity sub-narrative. At a certain point of the Project, some people worried that the Gadget might fizzle; and as a result the plutonium of the failed bomb might end up irrecoverably scattered around the test site. Recoverability of the plutonium was a concern because at a certain point of the Project it was thought that plutonium would in critically short supply for the foreseeable future; and the Gadget's plutonium was worth "several hundred million dollars".

> [Jumbo was] *a containment vessel for an unsuccessful explosion, For many of the Los Alamos scientists, Jumbo was the physical manifestation of the lowest point in the Laboratory's hopes for the success of an implosion bomb. The bomb would be placed into the heart of Jumbo, and if the bomb's detonation was unsuccessful, the outer walls of Jumbo would not be breached, making it possible to recover the bomb's plutonium.*
>
> (Wikipedia)

* * *

Jumbo - the Gadget's unused containment vessel.

Then there was a sudden change of plan.

> *After extensive research and testing of other potential containment ideas, the concept of Jumbo was decided on in the late summer of 1944. However, by the spring of 1945, after Jumbo had already been built and transported (with great difficulty) to the Trinity Site by the Eichleay Corporation of Pittsburgh, it was decided not to explode the Trinity device inside of Jumbo after all. There were several reasons for this new decision: first, plutonium had become more readily (relatively) available; second, the Project scientists decided that the Trinity device would probably work as planned; and last, the scientists realized that if Jumbo were used it would adversely affect the test results, and add 214 tons of highly radioactive material to the atmosphere.*

(National Atomic Museum)

That's the story. But maybe "by the spring of 1945" exactly the opposite situation prevailed. How confident were the scientists that "*the Trinity device would probably work as planned*"? Here's what a Manhattan Project physicist had to say about that, explaining his bet of zero yield for the Gadget in the pre-Trinity pool:

> *I bet zero. I think that was the most intelligent bet of any because zero included not only zero but it also included the first 25 generations of neutrons, and this is an exponentially growing thing, so it's probably the first 35 generations of neutrons. And if it stopped anywhere along there, it would be zero on the scale that they had. So I had, statistically, the best chance of winning.*
>
> (Nobel Laureate Norman Ramsey)

By the spring of 1945, the scientists realized that they'd have to stage a fake demonstration. In committing to that scenario, the idea of providing for a possible fizzle is absurd. The fizzle is not scripted into the fake-out. It would nullify the whole point of the Kabuki nuke exercise. Not only that, but having to intimately configure a fake bomb in, around, or beside a strong container like Jumbo complicates life. The fake (a large non-nuclear explosion) might not be powerful enough to totally destroy the container, as a good nuke should. But if Jumbo were to be set up at a "just so" distance (say, 800 yards) from the faked blast, the absence of damage might seem natural enough. Certainly nobody would quibble about a lack of total destruction (nobody did). The very strange official story about the placement was:

> ...the plan was to erect the vessel 800 yards from Ground Zero, so that it could stand ready to contain the next full-scale or partial-scale test.
>
> ('Critical Assembly' Hoddeson et al.)

A truly bizarre rationale. It's true that Jumbo wasn't easy to move, but situating it 800 yards away from a 20 kiloton nuclear blast is not keeping this expensive object "ready" and pristine for later use. If Jumbo was a lot of trouble to move, surely constructing a special mounting tower and hoisting it up in harm's way (even closer to the bomb's detonation altitude than if they'd just left it on the ground) was as much trouble. They could have protected it better (to keep it "ready") with much less trouble by just bulldozing some dirt over it. Anyway, Jumbo's mounting tower was blown apart by the test blast, and Jumbo came to rest on the desert floor. And there (having survived the Gadget's 'nuclear blast' as well as General Groves' 1946 attempt to have it demolished by high explosives), its mutilated carcass rests to the present day.

Jumbo sitting among the ruins of its 70 foot steel tower after the Trinity test. Note that the Jumbo tower might have been blown up in a separate and subsequent operation, as opposed to being a by-product of the main Trinity show.

100-Ton Test

It's not widely known that a baby blast test was conducted prior to the Gadget's real money shot. This is called the 100-Ton Test.

> A rehearsal was held on May 7, 1945, in which 108 short tons (96 long tons; 98 t) of high explosive spiked with radioactive isotopes were detonated.

> (Wikipedia)

Money Shot: TRINITY

20-foot high platform for 100-ton high explosive test.

Because there would be only one chance to carry out the test correctly, Bainbridge decided that a rehearsal should be carried out to allow the plans and procedures to be verified, and the instrumentation to be tested and calibrated. A 20-foot (6.1 m) high wooden platform was constructed 800 yards (732 m) to the south-east of Trinity ground zero and 108 long tons (110 t) of TNT were stacked on top of it. Flexible tubing was threaded through the pile of boxes of explosives. A radioactive slug from Hanford with 1,000 curies (37 TBq) of beta ray activity and 400 curies (15 TBq) of gamma ray activity was dissolved, and Hempelmann poured it into the tubing. The fireball of the conventional explosion was visible from Alamogordo Army Air Field 60 miles (97 km) away, but there was little shock at the base camp 10 miles (16 km) away. Shields thought that the explosion looked "beautiful", but it was hardly felt at 15,000 feet (4,572 m).

(Wikipedia)

Does this qualify as 'integration testing'? No. There were essentially no components of the actual Gadget used here. But notice that even this infinitely simpler test had, as we might expect, a glitch.

> *An electrical signal of unknown origin caused the explosion to go off 0.25 seconds early, ruining experiments that required split-second timing.*
>
> (Wikipedia)

Anything like this electrical error, which as stated above was never understood, diagnosed or corrected, would have completely trashed the real Trinity shot. Because the Gadget, far more than the 100-Ton 'experiments', crucially relied on split-second timing.

The 100-Ton test resulted in a 5-foot (1.52 m) deep and 30-foot (9.14 m) wide blast crater. Here is a shot of the Wiki page for this statement (in case it's changed later in response to this book):

MONEY SHOT: TRINITY

100-ton test [edit]

Because there would be only one chance to carry out the test correctly, Bainbridge decided that a rehearsal should be carried out to allow the plans and procedures to be verified, and the instrumentation to be tested and calibrated. Oppenheimer was initially skeptical, but gave permission, and later agreed that it contributed to the success of the Trinity test.[33]

Men stack crates of high explosives for the 100-ton test

A 20-foot (6.1 m) high wooden platform was constructed 800 yards (732 m) to the south-east of Trinity ground zero (33.67123°N 106.47229°W) and 108 long tons (110 t) of TNT were stacked on top of it. Kistiakowsky assured Bainbridge that the explosives used were not susceptible to shock. This was proven correct when some boxes fell off the elevator lifting them up to the platform. Flexible tubing was threaded through the pile of boxes of explosives. A radioactive slug from Hanford with 1,000 curies (37 TBq) of beta ray activity and 400 curies (15 TBq) of gamma ray activity was dissolved, and Hempelmann poured it into the tubing.[33][41][42]

The test was scheduled for May 5, but was postponed for two days to allow for more equipment to be installed. Requests for further postponements had to be refused because they would have impacted the schedule for the main test. The detonation time was set for 04:00 Mountain Daylight Time, also known as Mountain War time, on May 7, but there was a 37-minute delay to allow the observation plane,[43] a Boeing B-29 Superfortress from the 216th Army Air Forces Base Unit flown by Major Clyde "Stan" Shields,[44] to get into position.[43]

The fireball of the conventional explosion was visible from Alamogordo Army Air Field 60 miles (97 km) away, but there was little shock at the base camp 10 miles (16 km) away.[43] Shields thought that the explosion looked "beautiful", but it was hardly felt at 15,000 feet (4,572 m).[44] Herbert L. Anderson practiced using a converted M4 Sherman tank lined with lead to approach the 5-foot (1.52 m) deep and 30-foot (9.14 m) wide blast crater and take a sample of dirt, although the radioactivity was low enough to allow several hours of unprotected exposure. An electrical signal of unknown origin caused the explosion to go off 0.25 seconds early, ruining experiments that required split-second timing. The piezoelectric gauges developed by Anderson's team correctly indicated an explosion of 108 tons of TNT (450 GJ), but Luis Alvarez and Waldman's airborne condenser gauges were far less accurate.[41][45]

Description of the 100-Ton test and blast crater size (highlighted fragment).

I highlight the crater size in the Wiki screen shot for comparison when we get to the real Gadget show, just below. Note the radioactive spiking described for this test. In effect this was the first 'dirty bomb' (non-nuclear radiation scattering device). It may have been deemed desirable by May 1945 to pre-seed the test area with some confounding radioactivity in preparation for the big fake. Note that at the time, even scientists weren't sure how persistent explosively scattered radiation would turn out to be (witness the crazy-quilt of conflicting predictions and assessments later made regarding the Hiroshima aftermath).

As for the explosion itself, it's interesting that a nice sequence of color photos (or motion picture) was made . Unfortunately I can't reproduce the nice sunset hues here, but use your imagination to fill in lots of yellow, red, and orange.

83

100-Ton test explosion, color sequence.

Money Shot: TRINITY

The New York Times in a 2010 article reported; that: "*Nuclear specialists say the shape and size of a weapon['s explosion] ... can reveal design secrets.*" I would have thought so – that's why the test films were initially classified. The entire "100-Ton" frame sequence is usually offered, at Wikipedia and many other establishment sites, like Atomic Heritage Foundation, as historical research footage, a record of the 100-Ton test. At the same time, this exact footage appears in the 1947 film '*The Beginning or the End*' (a cheesy b/w docudrama about the Manhattan Project) – presented as a depiction of the actual Trinity gadget explosion. It's possible that (through film consultants Groves and Oppenheimer) the filmmakers got access to the real 100-Ton (originally classified) test footage, as Stanley Kubrick did in using 'real' test film for the finale of *Dr. Stranglove*. Or there may be some other confusion here.

In any case, there was said to be a color sequence of the 100-Ton test, from which I've selected three frames. By contrast, the vastly more instrumented and immeasurably more significant Gadget blow was not documented in color – apart from a single almost accidental snapshot by somebody who was not officially tasked as part of the core Trinity camera team.

> *Jack W. Aeby (August 16, 1923 – June 19, 2015) was an American environmental physicist most famous for having taken the only well-exposed color photograph of the first detonation of a nuclear weapon on July 16, 1945 at the Trinity nuclear test site in New Mexico. While color motion pictures of the Trinity test were made, most were badly overexposed or damaged due to the fireball's tendency to blister and solarize the film. Aeby was a civilian assigned to the Health Physics Group with Emilio Segrè at the time his snapshot was taken.*

>   (Wikipedia)

Without a reference for actual distance and expected yield, could you determine the fundamental difference between the two tests?

Death Object

The only color (use your imagination) photograph of the Gadget Just after the initial flash and 'dome' phase.

Of course, lying face-down feet-first to the blast at time zero doesn't aid fine-grain discernment either.

> *Everyone was told to lie face down on the ground, with his feet toward the blast, to close his eyes, and to cover his eyes with his hands as the countdown approached.*
>
> ('Now It Can Be Told' Leslie Groves)

Money Shot: TRINITY

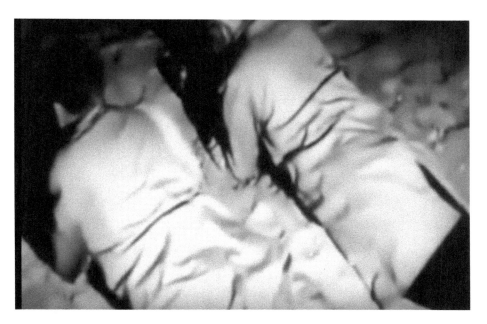

How to witness a nuke – feet first, face away.

If you think that further scaling up of a pseudo-nuke operation like the 100-Ton test would be impossible or unlikely, I see your complaint and raise you 'Sailor Hat'.

> *Operation Sailor Hat was a series of three tests of explosives effects, conducted by the United States Navy on the island of Kahoʻolawe, Hawaii in 1965. They were non–nuclear tests employing large quantities of conventional explosives (i.e. TNT) to simulate the effects of a nuclear weapon blast, such as the effects upon naval vessels. In addition, seismological data, underwater acoustics, radio communications, cratering, air blast effects, cloud growth, fireball generation, and electromagnetic data were gathered. Each "Sailor Hat" test consisted of a dome-stacked 500-ton (450 t) charge of TNT high explosive detonated on the shore of Kahoʻolawe.*
>
> (Wikipedia)

500 tons of TNT (20 × 40 feet) awaiting detonation at Operation Sailor Hat.

I Am Become Death

It is like some weird dream, conceived by one with too vivid an imagination.

(Abe Spitzer, radar operator of B-29 *The Great Artiste*, on viewing film of Trinity test explosion)

We finally arrive at the crown jewel of 'extraordinary evidence' - the dark saga's climax with the sci-fi weapon that was 'brighter than a thousand suns'. The Trinity Gadget test bomb was the ultra-complex design of implosion-triggered plutonium, nearly exact twin to Fat Man. Nothing remotely like this machine had ever been integration tested. The theory on which it was based was incomplete and poorly understood at best, or plain wrong. The key detonation timing component seemed to have failed just days before, or, speaking more properly, was for all practical purposes never properly component tested, as we saw earlier. Yet this thing functioned exactly to spec on its very first road test.

Here were the original test site selection criteria:

> *The Los Alamos scientists established the following criteria for the* [test shot] *site:*
>
> - *flat terrain to minimize effects of the blast and to facilitate easy construction of roads and communication lines;*
> - *sufficient distance from populated areas but close to Los Alamos to minimize travel between the two sites;*
> - *clear and sunny weather on average to permit the extensive collection of optical data;*
> - *and convenience to good rail transportation.*
>
> (Draft Final Report of CDC's LAHDRA Project)

Note: *"flat terrain to minimize effects of the blast"*. Yet later, Hiroshima was chosen partly for its flat terrain that would "maximize the effects of the blast".

Note *"clear and sunny weather to permit extensive collection of optical data"*. Yet for the actual test: *The preferred time was several hours before dawn* (Hoddeson et al. 1993). It ended up scheduled for pre-dawn darkness of 4 AM, with high-power spotlights set up to pinpoint the tower for aerial observation. It was delayed by weather concerns until 5:30 AM - when it was still dark.

> *At 05:29:21 MWT (± 2 seconds), the device exploded with an energy equivalent to around 20 kilotons of TNT (84 TJ). The desert sand, largely made of silica, melted and became a mildly radioactive light green glass, which was named trinitite. It left a crater in the desert 5 feet (1.5 m) deep and 30 feet (9.1 m) wide.* (Wikipedia)

DEATH OBJECT

A question arises about the crater. You'll notice it is cited as the same size as the crater from the 100-Ton test – 5 feet deep and 30 feet wide. I'm including the Wiki page here, in case of later change.

Detonation [edit]

The scientists wanted good visibility, low humidity, light winds at low altitude and westerly winds at high altitude for the test. The best weather was predicted between July 18 and 21, but the Potsdam Conference was due to start on July 16 and President Harry S. Truman wanted the test to be conducted before the conference began. It was therefore scheduled for July 16, the earliest date at which the bomb components would be available.[82]

The detonation was initially planned for 04:00 MWT but was postponed because of rain and lightning from early that morning. It was feared that the danger from radiation and fallout would be increased by rain, and lightning had the scientists concerned about a premature detonation.[83] A crucial favorable weather report came in at 04:45,[57] and the final twenty-minute countdown began at 05:10, read by Samuel Allison.[84] By 05:30 the rain had gone.[57] There were some communication problems. The shortwave radio frequency for communicating with the B-29s was shared with the Voice of America, and the FM radios shared a frequency with a railroad freight yard in San Antonio, Texas.[80]

Jack Aeby's still photo is the only known well-exposed color photograph of the detonation[71]

Trinitite

Two circling B-29s observed the test, with Shields again flying the lead plane. They carried members of Project Alberta, who would carry out airborne measurements during the atomic missions. These included Captain Deak Parsons, the Associate Director of the Los Alamos Laboratory and the head of Project Alberta; Luis Alvarez, Harold Agnew, Bernard Waldman, Wolfgang Panofsky and William Penney. The overcast obscured their view of the test site.[85]

At 05:29:21 MWT (± 2 seconds),[86] the device exploded with an energy equivalent to around 20 kilotons of TNT (84 TJ). The desert sand, largely made of silica, melted and became a mildly radioactive light green glass, which was named trinitite.[87] It left a crater in the desert 5 feet (1.5 m) deep and 30 feet (9.1 m) wide.[42] At the time of

Trinity detonation page on Wiki, with crater size highlighted at bottom.

We wonder why the craters were about the same size. There was a difference in the height of deployment – 20 feet up for the 100-Ton test vs. 100 feet for the Gadget. But the Gadget was **20,000 tons** of TNT equivalent – compared to 100 tons. It might be expected to have made more of a dent in the sand. Here's a ground level view of that crater:

Money Shot: TRINITY

A soldier examines one of the footings to the 100-foot steel tower at ground zero months after the test.

Trinity crater.

Here's another view:

Trinity 'crater' walk, featuring General Leslie Groves. It's not clear whether the lower dark horizontal line in background marks the shallow bomb crater lip or is a pre-existing feature on the site.

In 1946 the USA detonated a (supposed) nuclear device of comparable dimensions near Bikini atoll in the Pacific, as part of 'Operation Crossroads'.

> Operation Crossroads was a pair of nuclear weapon tests conducted by the United States at Bikini Atoll in mid-1946. They were the first nuclear weapon tests since Trinity in July 1945, and the first detonations of nuclear devices since the atomic bombing of Nagasaki on August 9, 1945. The purpose of the tests was to investigate the effect of nuclear weapons on warships.

(Wikipedia)

MONEY SHOT: TRINITY

The shot code-named Baker is described as follows:

> *In Baker on July 25, the weapon was suspended beneath landing craft LSM-60 anchored in the midst of the target fleet. Baker was detonated 90 feet (27 m) underwater, halfway to the bottom in water 180 feet (55 m) deep.*

(Wikipedia)

Baker's yield is estimated at 23 kilotons, vs. about 20+/- kilotons TNT equivalent for Trinity. So Baker wasn't all *that* wildly more powerful than Gadget. The Baker device was a Fat Man plutonium implosion-type nuclear weapon similar to that dropped on Nagasaki. Here was the supposed effect:

> *The result created a shallow crater on the seafloor 30 feet deep and nearly 2,000 feet wide.*

(Atomic Heritage Foundation)

If a 30-foot crater depth is 'shallow', what word applies to the Trinity test's 5-foot crater? Considering that both devices were nearly the same height above the surface (100 feet above desert for Gadget, 90 feet above sea floor for Baker), this discrepancy in crater depths is interesting. Perhaps that's due to the effect of water buffering (as a less compressive medium than air - but that could have functioned equally well to *protect* the sea floor). It's an interesting research problem.

It's possible that among all the details necessary to arrange for a good Trinity display, the crater size issue was overlooked. Or it may have been difficult to dip out a good size crater within the time and logistical parameters required by other parts of the operation (tower construction etc.) By the time of Baker' perhaps they were determined to fluff up this previously overlooked element of a good nuclear show with a more exaggerated report.

Death Object

September 1945: General Groves, Oppenheimer and other scientists inspecting Ground Zero.

Trinitite

Trinitite, also known as atomsite or Alamogordo glass, is the glassy residue left on the desert floor after the plutonium-based Trinity nuclear bomb test on July 16, 1945, near Alamogordo, New Mexico. The glass is primarily composed of arkosic sand composed of quartz grains and feldspar (both microcline and smaller amount of plagioclase with small amount of calcite, hornblende and augite in a matrix of sandy clay) that was melted by the atomic blast. It is usually a light green, although color can vary. It is mildly radioactive but safe to handle.

(Wikipedia)

The interesting thing about Tinitite is how little of it seems to be reported at other test sites. However, Trinitite or something very like it *is* found on earth, formed by natural causes. It's called *tektite*.

> *The glass is a form of tektite, a word which comes from the Greek word tektos, meaning molten. However, it is not known yet if tektites were first produced on the moon and then ejected as meteorites which landed on earth or whether they were produced as a result of an impact on earth. Another theory has it that the glass was not a result of a meteor impact but of a "radiative melting from meteoric aerial bursts"* **which makes the glass analogous to trinitite** *(which is created from sand blasted by thermal radiation of a nuclear explosion).*
>
> (www.sandia.gov/news/publications/technology/2006/0804/glass.html)

> *Planetary scientist Farouk El-Baz has just discovered "the largest crater yet found in the Sahara," and is suggesting that it has the right characteristics to answer a long-standing mystery.* **Since 1932, scientists have been picking up yellow-green glass in a 60-by-100-kilometer (35-by-60-mile) area of the desert of southern Egypt near the Libyan border.** *Study of the glass has revealed the unmistakable isotopic signature of an asteroid impact, but the source crater has never been found – until now.*
>
> (Science Magazine March 3, 2006)

There have been odd reports over the years of people claiming to have criminally broken through the Trinity site's security fence and scraped up all the trinitite into bags and truckloads for 'sacred re-burial' elsewhere. The Army is also said to have at some point dumped soil all over the flats, and there have been other reported shenanigans. Meanwhile, fake trinitite is widely available. Any conclusion on trinitite will have to wait for further research into other test sites, additional natural sites, and excavation and forensic analysis of the Trinity crater itself.

Fool Me Twice: Japan 1945

Hiroshima

Everything in a 2 mile radius of the explosion's epicenter was vaporized.

('The Manhattan Project: The Making of the Atomic Bomb' Al Cimino)

There you have it. 'Everything' was 'vaporized'. Including the people. But wait:

The [nuclear] scientist later became annoyed with me when I showed him a paper in which I had written that many people in Hiroshima were "vaporized" by the bomb. He pointed out that the correct term was "carbonized". "That's the problem with nonscientists: you are so sloppy with detail," he added.

('People of the Bomb' Hugh Gusterson)

Hmm… another multi-cultural moment. But I'm inclined to be more forgiving about that kind of sloppiness. Sometimes it's hard to know, in Marvin Gaye's immortal words, *what's going on*. Even when bodies aren't vaporized, merely carbonized, can we really be certain it was an effect of The Bomb? What would you say about the bodies in this photograph? Atomic carbonization? Or conventional napalm cooking?

FOOL ME TWICE: JAPAN 1945

Sci-fi *nuclear* carbonization of people?
Or merely *conventional* carbonization? You be the judge.

Little Boy

But before we get to the *really* horrifying stuff, let's back up to the boring question of testing once again, this time for a different device than the Trinity Gadget. If the Trinity test is the most impressive chunk of 'extraordinary evidence' for the (putative) existence of explosive fission chain reactions, the Little Boy uranium bomb 'gun' design lies (I use the term advisedly) at the other end of the scale. It is the most baffling and almost ridiculous 'just-so story' of the entire miserable nuclear saga.

Let's start with the bomb itself. Remember that the Trinity test's Gadget was the more complex plutonium implosion design. Little Boy was the much simpler uranium 'gun' design, as described in the previous chapter. What was the test track record of this 'Acme Atomic Bombs' device before combat use?

> *Although all of its components had been tested in target and drop tests, no full test of a gun-type nuclear weapon occurred before Hiroshima. There were several reasons for not testing a Little Boy type*

> of device. Primarily, there was insufficient uranium-235. Additionally, the weapon design was simple enough that it was only deemed necessary to do laboratory tests with the gun-type assembly. Unlike the implosion design, which required sophisticated coordination of shaped explosive charges, the gun-type design was considered almost certain to work. Thirty-two drop tests were conducted at Wendover, and only once did the bomb fail to fire. One last-minute modification was made, to allow the powder bags of propellant that fired the gun to be loaded in the bomb bay.
>
> (Wikipedia)

Note that the 'drop tests' referred to there were of dummies, not nuclear devices of course.

> In August 1944 Groves reported to the Top Policy Group that the scientists at Los Alamos were sufficiently confident of the uranium gun working that they advised it could be used in combat without a prior test.
>
> ('Brotherhood of the Bomb' Gregg Herken)

Little Boy was the first atomic weapon ever deployed in a battlespace. It wasn't just a matter of ramming some metal down a tube with a high explosive blast. It was to be the first explosive nuclear chain-reaction ever occurring in a deployed weapon, a phenomenon that, up to the moment that Little Boy shipped, was *a purely theoretical idea*. Note when Little Boy's parts shipped out:

> The target and bomb pre-assemblies (partly assembled bombs without the fissile components) left Hunters Point Naval Shipyard, California, on 16 July aboard the heavy cruiser USS Indianapolis.
>
> (Wikipedia)

This means that before Trinity, before there had ever been a fission explosion on planet Earth, Little Boy had begun its combat deployment. (The naughty bits followed a few days later on separate transport.) That's how confident the Project's tech team and brass were about a weapon that not only had never been used, and never been integration tested, but that was based on a theory that had never been tested either.

Here's one of the big reasons for the no-test thing, as cited in the Wikipedia entry: **Primarily, there was insufficient uranium-235**. 'Primarily'. Is it true?

> *By November 1944, all nine Alpha* racetracks [uranium enrichment facilities] *were running at full capacity – daily feeding more than 100 grams of U235 into two Beta tracks. Weekly shipments of enriched uranium to Los Alamos had begun. Just before Thanksgiving, Lawrence telephoned Groves from Oak Ridge to exult that "things are really booming down here." The production of U235 in November equaled all previous months combined. In December came another new record: nearly 200 grams of uranium, 80-percent pure U235, were left in the receivers after a single day's run. All nine Alpha tracks and three Beta tracks were in continuous operation for the first time.*
>
> ('Brotherhood of the Bomb' Gregg Herken)

Furthermore, if uranium supply was the only limitation on an otherwise proven, guaranteed, war-ending, world-beating weapon system, then research and production effort should have doubled or tripled on that, to the exclusion of any other activity. *It was wartime.*

But I shouldn't Monday-morning quarterback these guys too hard. After all, they were right - it worked straight from the box, as we'll see in the attack story further below. But let's think about the implications of this for a minute. First of all, we have to admire and applaud the Manhattan Project bomb designers. Not for making a fancy new-fangled sci-fi weapon, but for exactly the *opposite* achievement. They created something that fits a weapons guy's far more significant design goals: robust, reliable, unbreakable, practically field-strippable, and so on. That, not sophistication and complexity, is what makes a classic weapon design for the ages. The Little Boy device ranks right up with, indeed can only be compared to, the greatest weapons design triumph of the 20th century, (maybe even the GOAT - Greatest Of All Time) – the Kalashnikov rifle:

> *The AK-47, or AK as it is officially known (also known as the Kalashnikov) is a selective-fire (semi-automatic and automatic), gas-operated 7.62×39 mm assault rifle, developed in the Soviet Union by Mikhail Kalashnikov. Even after almost seven decades, the model and its variants remain* **the most popular and widely used assault rifles in the world because of their substantial reliability under harsh conditions, low production costs compared to contemporary Western weapons, availability in virtually every geographic region and ease of use.** *The AK-47 has been manufactured in many countries and has seen service with armed forces as well as irregular forces worldwide, and was the basis for developing many other types of individual and crew-served firearms. Of the estimated 500 million firearms worldwide, approximately 100 million belong to the Kalashnikov family, three-quarters of which are AK-47s.*
>
> (Wikipedia)

Now *that* is a weapons design for the ages. And if we believe the official story, the Little Boy was in this same elite realm of weapons that are preternaturally *"reliable, cheap, and easy to use"*. Just think: Little Boy, with no integration testing, relying on physics that had never been demonstrated, was shipped halfway around the world with god knows what kind of manhandling along the way, in wartime, bounced all over in its delivery vehicle, and functioned under unpredictable and variable parameters of temperature, moisture, altitude, vibration, etc. – functioned perfectly to spec.

To get a sense of the kind of thing that *could* have happened, consider the assembly of the Trinity Gadget (which was prepped under comparatively 'ideal' conditions).

Inserting the plug courted disaster, team member Boyce McDaniel re-members: "It was through [an opening] that the cylindrical plug containing the plutonium and initiator was to be inserted... In order to maximize the density of the uranium in the total assembly, the clearance between the plug and the spherical shell had been reduced to a few thousandths of an inch. Great care had been exercised to make sure... that mating pieces had been shipped to [Trinity]. Imagine our consternation when, as we started to assemble the plug in the hole, deep down in the center of the high explosive shell, it would not enter! Dismayed, we halted our efforts in order not to damage the pieces, and stopped to think about it. Could we have made a mistake...?"

Bacher saw the cause and calmed them: the plug had warmed and expanded in the hot ranch house but the tamper, set deep within the insulation of its shell of high explosives, was still cool from Los Alamos. The men left the two pieces of heavy metal in contact and took a break. When they checked the assembly again the temperatures had equalized. The plug slid smoothly into place.

('The Making of the Atomic Bomb' Richard Rhodes)

This kind of thing could easily have fouled up Little Boy somewhere along the line. The 'gun' design called for a cylindrical ring projectile to be fired onto a central spike of U235 metal. The sudden assembly was supposed to yield a critical mass that could be instantaneously triggered by a small neutron source. It was ballistically precise female-to-male instantaneous 'seating' or atomic sex if you will. These components had been jostled, bumped and man-handled thousands of miles over land, sea and air, and were now finally to be delivered all together from 30,000 feet altitude down to the detonation level around 2,000 feet. The temperature effects alone boggle the mind. Heat, cold, re-heating, refreezing – all kinds of things could have thrown these precise alignments out of whack at any point.

Suppose a commander, *in the middle of a war*, had a guaranteed supply of AK47 rifles - a battle rifle of incomparable ease and speed of deployment, as well as absolute reliability and versatility in the mud, crud, dirt and blood. Suppose this commander, about to take the field, knew all about the AK's superior economics of manufacture, training, and maintenance; and knew its brain-dead simple training, transport, field-stripping, cleaning and assembly. But then, a scientist came along and said:

Wait - I have the M16, a completely different, incompatible design that is vastly more finicky and troublesome. This is a new weapon with complex and unproven ballistics, it's much harder to disassemble and clean, far more likely to jam, and it uses a totally different ammo than what you've already begun to plan for. It might not work, as it needs an unspecified period of further development and invention. It can't just be banged out on a backyard ironworks, you need precise high-tech machine tools to manufacture it. How many shall I sign you up for?

What honest commander would turn his back on the AK, destroy all plans, and never look at it again? It smells more like concealing the evidence on a strictly Kabuki shell of an atomic 'weapon'. Basically it was abandoned after Hiroshima.

> *After the war ended, it was not expected that the inefficient Little Boy design would ever again be required, and many plans and diagrams were destroyed.*
>
> (Wikipedia)

Excuse me? This thing that cost umpteen billions in today's money, that functioned perfectly under combat conditions without integration testing, the very model of AK-style weapons design philosophy – and they *destroyed* plans and diagrams? They dumped it? No, wait. The "inefficient Little Boy" design, or that design family, was in fact manufactured for deployment, and the same basic type was (supposedly) fired off exactly 3 more times:

> (1) *A test firing of the W9 11-inch nuclear artillery shell in test shot Upshot-Knothole Grable on May 25, 1953*
>
> (Wikipedia)

> (2) *The W33 was an American nuclear artillery shell, fired from an eight-inch (203 mm) M110 howitzer and M115 howitzer. A total of 2,000 W33 projectiles were produced, the first of which was manufactured in 1957. The W33 remained in service until 1992. The W33 is the third known model of gun-type fission weapons to have been detonated as a test. The W33 was tested twice, first in Operation Plumbbob Laplace, on September 8, 1957 (yield of 1 kt), and the TX-33Y2 in Operation Nougat Aardvark on May 12, 1962, with a yield of 40 kilotons.*
>
> (Wikipedia)

So despite the fact that the tech specs and diagrams were destroyed, it was *reinvented* from scratch, was manufactured, and "remained in service" until 1992. This again shows how simple and perfect a design it was, that it was cobbled together again after being decommissioned and having its tech specs destroyed. The whole story of the 'gun' design bombs reminds me of Wile E. Coyote setting up for a shot at Roadrunner.

I'm sure there were good secret reasons for all these illogical actions and conflicting claims. So let's confine ourselves to the deeper question: was there no integration testing… because they were so sure it *would* work? Or because they'd become so sure it *wouldn't* work that they'd made other plans for staging a fake Japan atomic operation, and could relax about Little Boy's performance (assuming there even was any sincere attempt at a functional Little Boy in the first place)? There are two situations where no test is run: *when you know it works,* and *when you know it doesn't.*

Firestorm!

> *A firestorm is a conflagration which attains such intensity that it creates and sustains its own wind system. It is most commonly a natural phenomenon, created during some of the largest bushfires and wildfires. Although the word has been used to describe certain large fires, the phenomenon's determining characteristic is a fire with its*

> *own storm-force winds from every point of the compass. The Black Saturday bushfires and the Great Peshtigo Fire are examples of forest fires with some portion of combustion due to a firestorm. Firestorms can also occur in cities, usually as a deliberate effect of targeted explosives such as occurred as a result of the aerial firebombings of Hamburg, Dresden, and the atomic bombing of Hiroshima.*
>
> (Wikipedia)

The Hiroshima firestorm probably caused more damage than the blast itself. The general effect of a firestorm (for example, in Dresden) has been explained as follows:

> *Consider the use of precision saturation (incendiary) bombing in Dresden. At 10:09 AM, the first bombs were dropped unleashing a massive firestorm. Gigantic masses of air were then sucked in by the expanding inferno creating something similar to a tornado. People caught in this wind were mercilessly tossed into the flame, while those seeking protection underground suffocated as the fire gasped for more oxygen. The least fortunate were those who died from a blast of white heat which has temperatures so high it literally melts human skin.*
>
> (Eric Roberts)

Novelist Kurt Vonnegut Jr., who was present in Dresden at the time, commented:

> *You guys burnt the place down, turned it into a single column of flame. More people died there in the firestorm, in that one big flame, than died in Hiroshima and Nagasaki combined.*

Another analyst comments:

> *How and why, for more than half a century, did the U.S. government fail to predict nuclear fire damage as it drew up plans to fight strategic*

Fool Me Twice: Japan 1945

> *nuclear war? U.S. bombing in World War II caused massive fire damage to Hiroshima and Nagasaki, but later war plans took account only of damage from blast; they completely ignored damage from atomic firestorms. Recently a small group of researchers has shown that for modern nuclear weapons the destructiveness and lethality of nuclear mass fire often–and predictably–greatly exceeds that of nuclear blast.*
> (Whole World on Fire: Organizations, Knowledge, and Nuclear Weapons Devastation (Cornell Studies in Security Affairs))

They ask a good question. Why minimize nuclear-ignited firestorms? The problem is that firestorms can arise from causes other than nuclear, and have effects that are all too similar to supposed nuclear outcomes. It seems the brass at the time were anxious that nobody start to line up and too closely compare the 'atomic' outcomes against those of conventional firebombing raids.

> *Beginning with an incendiary raid on Tokyo on 9 March 1945 which Japanese records showed killed 83,793 and burned out 267,000 buildings (25% of Tokyo's buildings), sixty-four Japanese cities were destroyed by non-nuclear air raids. The detailed and objective analysis of these incendiary air raids was classified "Restricted" in April 1947 by the U.S. Strategic Bombing Survey in its unpublished limited distribution typeset and printed report Number 90, Effects of Incendiary Bomb Attacks on Japan; Part 3 (pages 65-118) documents the effects of the 9 March 1945 Tokyo incendiary raid, with photos on pages 104-109 very similar to the damage in Hiroshima and Nagasaki (combustible light frame buildings burned out with their steel distorted by the fires, and piles of charred bodies in streets). By omitting to publish this, an objective comparison of nuclear with conventional attacks was prevented.*
> ('The effects of the atomic bomb on Hiroshima, Japan'
> - U.S. Strategic Bombing Survey report)

In fact, the damage patterns of the supposed atomic attacks were nearly identical to previously observed firestorm effects.

DEATH OBJECT

> *Although fashionable books on Hiroshima tend to print pictures of the "blasted" twisted metal beams of the Odamasa Store (former Taiyo Theatre), USSBS building 52 at 2,800 feet from ground zero, page 322 explains it is an effect of fire: "Severe distortion caused by burning of combustible construction and contents." Furthermore, similar twisting of metal frames in wooden buildings occurred in the Tokyo incendiary attack, but those photos remained Restricted. It is not a special "nuclear" effect, nor are the burned bodies in the streets of Tokyo photographed after the main non-nuclear attack, despite all the polemic and inaccurate claims attacking civil defense.*
> (U.S. Strategic Bombing Survey)

Anyway let's get back to nature for a moment, let's talk trees.

Damaged trees at Nagasaki 2,700 feet southwest of ground zero.

This picture is described as follows by conventional histories:

> *Fat Man snapped trees at Nagasaki; the less powerful Hiroshima bomb only knocked them down.*
>
> ('The Making of the Atomic Bomb' Richard Rhodes)

There are spindly looking tree remnants to the right side of that Nagasaki picture which appear not only unsnapped, but still upright. What, other than a massive atomic blast of 20 kilotons (Fat Man), could have 'snapped' (or maybe we should say 'splintered') those trees? A firestorm, that's what.

> *Exploding trees occur when stresses in a tree trunk increase leading to an explosion. Exploding trees occur during forest fires and are a risk to smokejumpers. In Australia, the native eucalyptus trees are known to explode during bush fires due to the high flammability of vaporized eucalyptus oil produced by the tree naturally.*
>
> (Wikipedia)

The Nagasaki trees photo looks a lot like the usual jumbled mix of upright, damaged, toppled, and snapped wood that you see in the aftermath of any major forest fire.

Aftermath of an ordinary forest fire showing a jumbled mix of upright, splintered, snapped, and toppled trees.

Jumbled aftermath of the 1910 Big Blowup forest fire in Idaho.

That does not completely rule out a nuclear blast. After all, by conventional hypothesis, nuclear detonations themselves actually produce firestorms at some point (presumably even when not helped along by residential cooking and kitchen fires, as well as electrical shorts). But it shows that nuclear explosion need not be fixed on as the only possible cause of that kind of damage. With those photos as reference, let's look at blown-up Hiroshima.

DEATH OBJECT

Hiroshima near ground zero: a lot of vertical stuff...

There we see, close to ground zero, a bunch of utility poles in the foreground and tree remnants in the background. Not much of this skinny stuff has been 'knocked down'. Would 5 more kilotons have done the job? Maybe not, because you sometimes hear that vertical standing objects, when perfectly located 'just so' with respect to the blast, have remarkable superpowers:

> *Because the shock-front came down from almost directly overhead, telephone poles and trees... were able to resist and were largely bypassed by the forces of compression. Trees and poles and up-thrusting steel beams behaved much like the noses and fins of rocket bombs cutting through supersonic air.*
>
> ('The Last Train from Hiroshima' Charles Pellegrino)

It's amazing that so many scrawny, bent and twisted natural objects, located all over the blast area, as well as many dozens of utility poles, could all have been situated in the mathematically perfect angular centering with reference to the bottom of the blast front, such that this theoretically well-motivated 'vertical resistance' effect applied so extensively. But anything is possible. Maybe the exact zone pictured above matched perfectly with the overhead shock-front. Thus, maybe it's better not to consider trees and poles standing 'too close' to air zero, as it seems that may be the safest place for them. The problem is that as we move away from ground zero, we *still* find lots of standing trees and other vertical objects:

Hiroshima damage.

Again we see the familiar mixture of upright, leaning, and toppled trees and poles.

Plenty bad fire damage, yet upright trees are numerous along the left side of the central road.

So it seems that uprights are protected by the contradictory conditions of (i) being directly under 'air zero' and also, paradoxically, by being (ii) farther away - yet in zones from which most buildings were supposedly blasted down. But there must have been *some* kind of blast – if a real nuke was dropped. Let's tighten the bolts on the blast thing. At the 'air zero' detonation altitude of 600 meters, there would be an inner blast contour of 20 psi, and an outer contour of 5 psi effects. These are shown as concentric circles on the Hiroshima effects map.

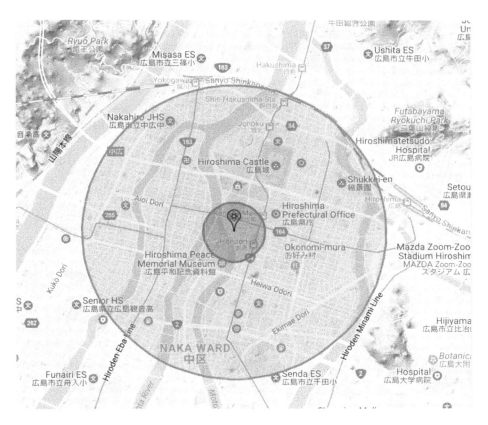

Diagram of Little Boy 15-kiloton air blast contours overlaid on (modern) Hiroshima. The inner circle is the 20 psi contour; the outer circle is the 5 psi contour. (see Bibliography for source attribution of the map and the overlay)

Here are descriptions of blast effects within the contours (note that Little Boy detonated at 600 meters, almost the theoretical ideal for maximal destruction).

Air blast radius (20 psi): 340 m (0.36 km²)

At 20 psi overpressure, heavily built concrete buildings are severely damaged or demolished; fatalities approach 100%.

Air blast radius (5 psi): 1.67 km (8.78 km²)

At 5 psi overpressure, most residential buildings collapse, injuries are universal, fatalities are widespread.

20 psi has a maximum wind speed of about 502 mph and 5 psi has a maximum wind speed of about 163 mph. The Hiroshima damage photos in this section are all from either the inner (20 psi) contour or at least the outer (5 psi) contour. It isn't necessarily true that psi decreases linearly and smoothly from the 20 psi center zone out to the 5 psi edge. But there must have been a pretty wide belt of, say, 10 psi, with wind speeds of up to 294 mph. On the Saffir-Simpson Hurricane Wind Scale:

> *A category 5 hurricane is the highest level of 'Major', defined as 157 mph or higher wind speeds: catastrophic damage will occur: A high percentage of framed homes will be destroyed, with total roof failure and wall collapse. Most trees will be snapped or uprooted and power poles downed.*
>
> (www.nhc.noaa.gov/aboutsshws.php)

So keep in mind, as you read on, that even the outer edge of the 5 psi contour should have experienced buffeting at, or exceeding, the highest level of hurricane force.

Seversky

Alexander P. de Seversky (June 7, 1894 – August 24, 1974) was a Russian-American aviation pioneer, inventor, and influential advocate of strategic air power. He made an inspection tour of Hiroshima and Nagasaki soon after the war's end. His observations and conclusions are particularly valuable as he had extensive personal experience in bombing and aerial warfare, as well as a deep conceptual and theoretical understanding of explosives and blast effects. His trip report was published in a 1946 magazine article, which was reprised at greater depth as a chapter in his 1950 book *'Air Power: Key to Survival'*.

Seversky is sometimes charged with bias. It's sometimes said that he misleadingly minimized atomic weapons' horrifying power, the better to either forestall or assuage American public guilt over dropping the bomb on prostrate Japan.

That's a ridiculous charge because in 1946 there was precious little guilt to worry about. The public overwhelmingly approved the bomb's use.

The American public thoroughly approved the bomb's use.

Nor was there much fear to calm. The USA was the sole possessor of nuclear weapons. It's more likely that Seversky's observations were exactly what they come across as – the candidly stated assessment of a rational, sober and highly knowledgeable military man (who believed implicitly in the existence of the atom bomb, and who merely disputed some of the hype about its effects). This report did little to endear him to an American political regime eager to instill fear in new post-war adversaries.

> After visiting the major areas of the Pacific, I arrived in Japan. I began the study to which I had been assigned by making an aerial tour of the islands of Honshu and Kyushu, which encompass the main portion of industrial Japan. I flew over Tokyo, Yokohama, Yokosuka, Nagoya, Osaka, Kobe, Akashi, and dozens of other towns and cities which had been subject to intensive air attack. Some of these towns are so close together that they seem almost continuous industrial sites.
>
> All of these areas of annihilation presented approximately the same visual pattern. The smaller towns were totally burned out. Seen from above the prevailing color was pinkish – the effect produced by the piles of ashes and rubble mixed with rusted metal. Similar pinkish carpets were spread out in the larger cities, except that among them stood large and small modern concrete buildings and factory structure, unscathed bridges, and other objects that had withstood the impact. Many of the buildings, of course, were gutted by fire, but this was not apparent from the air.
>
> I was keyed up for my first view of an atom-bombed city, prepared for the radically new sights suggested by the exciting descriptions I had read and heard. But to my utter astonishment, Hiroshima from the air looked exactly like all the other burned-out cities I had observed!
>
> There was a familiar pink blot, about two miles in diameter. It was dotted with charred trees and telephone poles. Only one of the city's twenty bridges was down. Hiroshima's clusters of modern buildings in the downtown section stood upright. It was obvious that the blast could not have been so powerful as we had been led to believe. It was extensive blast rather than intensive. I had heard of buildings instantly consumed by unprecedented heat. Yet here I saw the buildings structurally intact, and what is more, topped by undamaged flag poles, lightning rods, painted railings, air raid precaution signs and other comparatively fragile objects.

Fool Me Twice: Japan 1945

At the T-bridge, the aiming point for the atomic bomb, I looked for the "bald spot" where everything presumably had been vaporized in the twinkling of an eye. It wasn't there or anywhere else. I could find no traces of unusual phenomena. What I did see was in substance a replica of Yokohama or Osaka, or the Tokyo suburbs - the familiar residue of an area of wood and brick houses razed by uncontrollable fire. Everywhere I saw the trunks of charred and leafless trees, burned and unburned chunks of wood. The fire had been intense enough to bend and twist steel girders and to melt glass until it ran like lava - just as in other Japanese cities.

The concrete buildings nearest to the center of explosion, some only a few blocks from the heart of the atom blast, showed no structural damage. Even cornices, canopies and delicate exterior decorations were intact. Window glass was shattered, of course, but single-panel frames held firm; only window frames of two or more panels were bent and buckled. The blast impact therefore could not have been unusual.

(Reader's Digest 1946 Alexander P. de Seversky)

There is no mention of any kind of blast crater under 'air zero'. It may be that the detonation altitude was too great for that (1,900 feet). It also may be that in a built-up enemy city even a shallow crater is difficult to fudge, fake, or dig on short notice. Anywhere within *either* blast ring, you'd expect trees – if nothing else - to be pretty much wiped clean off the earth, vaporized, flung around like toothpicks in a hurricane, except possibly where shielded by concrete buildings.

Quite a number of plants not only remained upright, but actually *survived* in the most intense areas, to bloom again the following year.

A-bombed trees are trees that survived the atomic bombing of 6 August 1945. Some 170 trees, in 55 locations within the roughly 2km radius of the hypocenter, are officially registered by Hiroshima Municipality as A-bombed trees. Lovingly cared for over the years by authorities, botanists, various citizens' groups and individuals, they are identified

> by a name plate and the unique reference: hibakujumoku (survivor tree). These survivors of nuclear tragedy carry a significant message - not just for those living in or visiting Hiroshima, but for all of humanity.
>
> (United Nations Institute for Training and Research)

Maybe this book embodies the plants' 'significant message'.

What's Going On?

If the Trinity test is the most *intellectually* demanding event confronting the nuclear skeptic, then dealing with the accounts of people on the ground who actually suffered and died in these events (whatever caused them) is the greatest *emotional* challenge.

I don't have space to go deeply into the body count game. There are a variety of estimates of how many dead, wounded, sickened, and a lot of quibbling about what killed who when. Estimates can differ by many tens of thousands depending on your starting assumptions and methodology. Not to mention that everybody brings some kind of minimization or maximization bias to the table. Suffice it to say it's all plenty damn horrible no matter how you slice it. And it's all plenty damn horrible no matter how it was done – by science or fire, by land, sea or air. War is hell – nobody is disputing *that*.

But I have to keep tracking my technical subject - the FAIL hypothesis. So I won't be talking much about, say, the real population figures for Hiroshima in early August 1945 (pre-attack). Some accounts say the starting population was greatly exaggerated and that because of evacuations and lack of shipping activity in the port, the city had largely emptied out. At the very least, initial population estimates should take into account that after years of urban air attacks, most cities had been partially evacuated.

> Overall, 8.5 million Japanese civilians were displaced as a result of the American raids, including 120,000 of Hiroshima's population of 365,000 who evacuated the city before the atomic bomb attack on it in August 1945. (Wikipedia)

That estimate cuts against the grain of the usual fable about pre-attack Hiroshima as some kind of idyllic island of peace in the sea of flames that otherwise engulfed Japanese cities at the time. It's sometimes said that the residents of Hiroshima lived almost as normal nearly to the end, with only a weird feeling of invulnerability due to having been 'spared' up to that point. But accounts in some Japanese sources tell of a largely emptied city, with work details pulling down houses for firebreaks ('Clearance Project') and other somewhat spiritless civil defense activities predominating. Whatever the case, I can't get into all that.

There are some very impressive collections of heartbreaking survivor testimonies, beginning with the 1959 book 'Children of the A-Bomb' (English language edition) by Dr. Arata Osada. This book contains over sixty terrible first-person narratives from children on the ground. Most of them date from 1951. So presumably there were obstacles delaying Dr. Osada's publication. The soul-searing accounts of loss, desolation, and destruction wouldn't paint the American occupiers in the kindliest light. Many of these have a close variation of the following line in the first paragraph:

> *Just as we saw a bright flash there was a loud bang and I almost fainted.*
>
> (Sanae Kanoh, 5th grade girl)

These lines fit the profile as given by standard histories. Some of them have some interesting twists though:

> *I often heard the words, 'Air raids' and 'The war' and I remember them clearly. 'Today evacuation, tomorrow evacuation.' And then every day we wandered around places we had never seen before searching for a safe place to live. Those who didn't have any acquaintances in the country finally returned to the city. We were living in Hakushima. ... Mother and my three older sisters and I seated day after day at digging a shelter to which we would entrust the lives of the five of us. In July*

> *the air raids became more frequent and by the middle of the month they came as though by schedule. At half-past eight in the evening the air raids began, accompanied by the rasping sound from the radio. Each one with his particular belongings in hand jumped down into the shelter… Every time, praying in our hearts that we would all continue to be safe, we would wait for the dawn. When morning comes and the all-clear sounds, we all crowd out of the shelter.*
>
> (Masataka Asaeda, 9th grade boy)

This is bad enough, but it does not seem entirely compatible with the usual 'reserved city' narrative. Maybe this boy's account wasn't edited quite heavily enough leaving it out of alignment with the book's overall orientation.

> *The Atomic Bomb Survivors Relief Law defines hibakusha as people who fall into one or more of the following categories: within a few kilometers of the hypocenters of the bombs; within 2 km of the hypocenters within two weeks of the bombings; exposed to radiation from fallout; or not yet born but carried by pregnant women in any of these categories. The Japanese government has recognized about 650,000 people as hibakusha. As of March 31, 2016, 174,080 are still alive, mostly in Japan. The government of Japan recognizes about 1% of these as having illnesses caused by radiation.*
>
> (Wikipedia)

Many of the book's children fall under the second provision of the *hibakusha* specification: '*within 2 km of the hypocenters within two weeks of the bombings*'. That's because many of the respondents were not in the city at the time of the attack, as they had been evacuated. But most of them had homes and relatives in the city. Beyond this pioneering book, decades later there is now a web-based archive of over 3,000 very similar accounts by *hibakusha* (被爆者 atomic bomb victims).

Fool Me Twice: Japan 1945

What can be concluded? In a way, it's simple: either (i) nukes work as advertised and Little Boy wiped out Hiroshima in an instant, or (ii) the attack was a nuclear psy-op painted over the canvas of a real incendiary and high explosive attack. One or the other is the truth. If the former, it is interesting that after the first paragraph of these reports, the bulk of the material is always perfectly compatible with the horrors of WWII incendiary and high explosive air raids, as experienced all over Europe and Japan up to that time.

> On 13 February 1945, Victor Gregg was a 25-year-old British rifleman being held by the Germans in the beautiful city of Dresden. At about 10.30 pm, the air-raid sirens started wailing, and because this happened every night no notice was taken. But after a short period of silence, a wave of pathfinders started to drop target flares. We saw them ... filling the sky with blinding light, dripping burning phosphorus on to the streets and houses. The flares were still falling when the initial stream flew over, dropping thousands of incendiaries along with the first bombs. ... and the sky changed from a bright white to a dull red ... about four incendiaries burst through our glass roof... shredding the luckless men beneath. The phosphorus clung to the bodies of the injured, turning them into human torches,... and their screaming was added to the other cries....
>
> Suddenly, a "blockbuster" dropped outside our building, blowing in the whole wall. (These thin-walled, massive missiles could demolish whole blocks with one explosion, hence the name.) I was thrown nearly 50ft and covered in brickwork and rubble... the smoke and fumes from the building's burning shell were now being swept away by a gradually rising wind.... Wherever I turned, I was confronted with flames, smoke and dust – and all the time blocks of debris falling from the sky... Survivors were clawing their way through mounds of rubble that an hour before had been their homes. We stumbled along the remains of a wide avenue, flanked by fires and mountains of red-hot wreckage. (I was saved by my wooden soles, which were so thick that I could walk over the glowing cinders.) .. .. The new bombs were so big that you could see them in the sky. Even the incendiaries were different – not metre-long

sticks, but four-ton objects that exploded on the ground, incinerating anything within a radius of 200ft – and raining down with these came more blockbusters, 10-tonners this time.

Everything was in flames, even the roads, which were burning rivers of bubbling and hissing tar. Huge fragments of material flew through the air, sucked into the vortex. We could see people being torn from whatever they were hanging on to and drawn into the ever-deepening red glow less than 200 yards away. A small group tried to reach us by crossing what had once been a road, only to get themselves stuck in a bubbling mass of molten tar. One by one, they sank to the ground through sheer exhaustion and then died in a pyre of smoke and flame. People of all shapes, sizes and ages were slowly sucked into the vortex, then suddenly whisked into the pillars of smoke and fire, their hair and clothing alight. ..above the wind's howl and the inferno's roar came the interminable, agonised screams of the victims being roasted alive. ... It was a sea of flame rising into a sky of smoke. .. When the raid ended, we continued with the cellars, prising them open .. Inside, we found the victims' bodies, usually shrivelled to half their normal size or worse. (Children under the age of three or four had simply melted.)

Some of the corpses were so brittle that they crumbled into clouds of ash and dried flesh. We set off to a small square, where what had been grass was now a bed of ash 4in thick, and the first three shelters we uncovered were empty. Trudging through streets where sheets of flame were still shooting up 100ft, we came to the door of a communal shelter, which took all afternoon to prise open. .. a terrible smell hit us – and slowly the horror inside became visible. There were no real, complete bodies, only bones and scorched articles of clothing matted together on the floor and stuck together by a sort of jelly. There was no flesh visible, just a glutinous mass of solidified fat and bones, inches thick, on the floor.

('Dresden, a Survivor's Story' Victor Gregg)

That kind of thing is pretty much what you read in 'Children of the A-Bomb', following the initial 'standardized' paragraph of each report.

If, on the other hand, the FAIL hypothesis is true, then the first paragraph of each account in 'Children of the A-Bomb' has been consciously or unconsciously edited to bring it into line with atomic gospel. After the Occupation ended, there may have been less pressure to keep the USA military looking good, and more emphasis on building an international image for Japan of striving for peace and human harmony etc. The unique suffering described in the 'A-Bomb' book – whatever caused it - certainly worked towards that end, because most of the reports conclude with a somewhat formulaic plea for peace and renunciation of weapons and war forever. Make it so!

One of the most interesting stories of adult survival is the saga of Kenji Hirata, who by ill or good luck lived to tell about *both* the atomic attacks of August, 1945. After losing his wife in the Hiroshima bombing, he caught a train over to Nagasaki and managed to live through the second bombing there. Hirata's amazing experience is illuminating because it plumbs the depths and tests the boundaries of virtually every dimension of this historically complex event – time, space, physics, logistics, and raw human emotion.

Hirata's story has been movingly rendered by author Charles Pellegrino in his book '*The Last Train from Hiroshima*'. In a nutshell, Hirata was working in the Hiroshima area that morning at a plant four kilometers distant from ground zero. He survived the blast, though it was a very close call. However, Setsuko, his new bride, was unfortunately at their home downtown, almost directly beneath 'air zero' - the detonation point. She was vaporized and their house was destroyed. After somewhat recovering himself that morning, Hirata bravely ventured into the firestorm, heading to his house to find his wife. When he arrived at the site, no trace of her could be found. A few neighbors who had survived by lucky accidents of positioning explained what had happened there, so close to ground zero. Realizing that the situation was hopeless, Hirata resolved to gather a few fragments of material representing his wife's remains and to return with them to the couple's original hometown – Nagasaki. He took a train from Hiroshima and arrived in Nagasaki in time to experience and survive the second bombing. He later remarried and lived quietly for many years, avoiding publicity and keeping his almost unique experience untold until Pellegrino brought it to the world in the last years of Hirata's life.

It began for Hirata that morning at his workplace:

> *Kenshi had been working as an accountant at the Mitsubishi Weapons Plant, slightly **more than four kilometers** [2.5 miles] away. A young woman nearby had crept to a window and peeked outside. Whatever she saw in the direction of the city, Kenshi would never know. She stood up, uttered something guttural and incomprehensible, and then the blast wave—lagging far behind the bomb's light waves—caught up with her. By the time the windowpanes traveled a half-meter, they had separated completely from their protective cross-hatched net of air-raid tape, emerging as thousands of tiny shards. Like the individual pellets of a shotgun blast, each shard had been accelerated to more than half the speed of sound. The girl at the window took at least a quarter-kilogram of glass in her face and her chest before the wind jetted her toward the far wall. Kenshi did not see where she eventually landed. Simultaneous with the window blast, the very floor of the building had come off its foundation and bucked him more than a half-meter into the air.*
>
> ('Surviving the Last Train From Hiroshima: The Poignant Case of a Double Hibakusha' Charles Pellegrino)

The exact location of the Mitsubishi plant relative to Hiroshima city topography isn't given, but note the extreme power of these terrifying effects at four kilometers distance: *"blast wave"*, *"windowpanes traveled a half meter"*, *"shotgun blast"*, *"half the speed of sound"*, *"wind jetted her toward the far wall"*, *"floor [came] off its foundation"*, *"bucked him more than a half-meter into the air"*. It was an almost unsurvivable impact. The speed of sound is 767 mph. Half that is 383 mph. 10 psi impact is equivalent to 294 mph winds. The blast here was hitting with well over 10 psi pressures, nearly twice the threshold of a Category 5 hurricane, which begins at 157 mph. Fortunately Hirata came through it all right, having ducked down behind cover at the last moment.

2.3 miles (3.7 kilometers) from hypocenter
Isao Kita.
Age at impact: 33 years old

KITA: *Well, at that time, I happened to be receiving the transmission over the wireless. I was in the receiving room and I was facing northward. I noticed the flashing light. It was not really a big flash. But still it drew my attention. In a few seconds, the heat wave arrived. After I noticed the flash, white clouds spread over the blue sky. It was amazing. It was as if blue morning-glories had suddenly bloomed up in the sky. It was funny, I thought. Then came the heat wave. It was very very hot. Even though there was a window glass in front of me, I felt really hot. It was as if I was looking directly into a kitchen oven. I couldn't bear the heat for a long time. Then I heard the cracking sound. I don't know what made that sound, but probably it came from the air which suddenly expanded in the room.*

By that time, I realized that the bomb had been dropped. As I had been instructed, I pushed aside the chair and lay with my face on the floor. Also as I had been instructed during the frequent emergency exercises, I covered my eyes and ears with hands like this. And I started to count. You may feel that I was rather heartless just to start counting. But for us, who observed the weather, it is a duty to record the process of time, of various phenomena. So I started counting with the light flash. When I counted to 5 seconds, I heard the groaning sound. At the same time, the window glass was blown off and the building shook from the bomb blast. So the blast reached that place about 5 seconds after the explosion.

(Hiroshima Peace Cultural Center and NHK)

Kita's testimony above is one of the most interesting. It almost seems he had prior knowledge of a single super bomb and its features. The 'count' that he talks about would not be especially relevant in the case of anything Japan had experienced up to that point. Furthermore, he says *"as I had been instructed… I lay with my face on the floor. … I covered my eyes and ears with my hands"*. The actions taken by Kita are very much like the instructions to the Trinity witnesses. I have never read that kind of account of a Japanese wartime emergency drill. Normally they were concerned first and foremost with evacuation:

"During World War II, we [ran and] hid in air raid shelters wearing masks when we heard the sirens," said Reinosuke Ishigaki, an 89-year old resident.

(CNN March 19, 2017)

2.54 miles (4.1 kilometers) from hypocenter
Hiroshi Sawachika.
Age at impact: 28 years old

SAWACHIKA: *I was in my office. I had just entered the room and said "Good morning." to colleagues and I was about to approach my desk when outside it suddenly turned bright red. I felt very hot on my cheeks. Being the chief of the room, I shouted to the young men and women in the room that they should evacuate. As soon as I cried, I felt weightless as if I were an astronaut. I was then unconscious for 20 or 30 seconds. When I came to, I realized that everybody including myself was lying at one side of the room. Nobody was standing. The desks and chairs had also blown off to one side. At the windows, there was no window glass and the window frames had been blown out as well.*

(Hiroshima Peace Cultural Center and NHK)

Now let's pick up the trail with Hirata again. Two days after the atomic attack on Hiroshima, he took a train departing from Koi Station heading for Nagasaki. Koi Station is located 2.29 kilometers from the Hiroshima hypocenter – much closer than Hirata's workplace to ground zero, about half the distance.

Fool Me Twice: Japan 1945

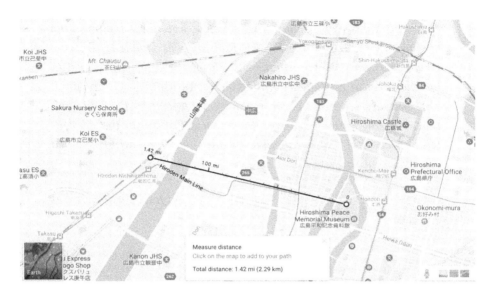

Koi Station is 2.29 kilometers from hypocenter.

We can't expect blast effects to be strictly linear with distance, and particularly not in a heterogeneous urban landscape. But, while blast effects could vary widely depending on a building's exact orientation, construction, and intervening structures, still we do find an extreme contrast between the supposed effects on Hirata's workplace compared to the situation at Koi Station – half the distance from the hypocenter:

> During the war, today's Nishihiroshima Station, run by the Japan Railway Company, was called Koi Station, and Hiroden Nishihiroshima Station, run by the Hiroshima Electric Railway, was called Nishihiroshima Station or Koi. Both stations were about 2.4 km from the hypocenter. According to the Record of the Hiroshima A-bomb Disaster, Koi Station, part of the National Railway back then, was largely destroyed in the A-bomb blast. The 20 or 30 staff members of the station crept out from the wreckage to the train tracks. Because of the black rain that fell in the aftermath, damage from fire was minimal. As the bomb was dropped after both the inbound and outbound trains had left the station before 8 a.m., there were few passengers in the station at the time. The Sanyo Line was restored by the

National Railway on August 8. A streetcar line, the Miyajima Line operated by the Hiroshima Electric Railway, was unable to continue service between Nishihiroshima and Kusatsu Station on August 6, but the streetcar continued running between Kusatsu and Miyajima. The next day, streetcars began running end to end on the Miyajima Line, carrying many survivors. Another streetcar line in the city center, between Koi and Nishitenma (present-day Tenmacho) resumed operations on August 9.

(Chugoku News Service)

Koi station A-bomb damage. Trestle bridge and tracks apparently unscathed, and reported to be fit for use 48 hours post-blast.

Some station staff may possibly have been killed, but there is no mention of fatalities. Given that "20 or 30" personnel are mentioned as surviving, we can assume staff casualties were not significant. That conclusion is supported by the rapidity with which inter-city service on the Sanyo line was restored. Trains were apparently running in and out by the next day but one. That conclusion in turn is supported by the photographic evidence, showing little apparent damage to the complex trestle and track structure. This is an amazing outcome, given what happened at twice the distance from ground zero, as we've seen in the testimonials.

By contrast with the Hiroshima case, after the 1995 Kobe earthquake (magnitude 6.9) the New York Times reported: *Railroad officials estimate it will take at least three months to repair tracks and bridges.*

> *An earthquake of Richter scale 6.0 releases energy of ~15 kilotons – which is the approximate yield of the Little Boy atomic bomb dropped on Hiroshima (~16 kt).*
>
> (Wikipedia: 'TNT equivalent for seismic energy yield')

It's true that earthquakes of 6.9 magnitude are much worse than 6.0 magnitude quakes. And presumably they're much worse than "16 kt" atom bombs (which are intentionally designed, deployed, and deliberately targeted by enemies to destroy things... hmm). And an earthquake affects a wider area. So let's cut that 90-day (minimum) repair estimate massively - by a factor of 10. Nine days is still significantly longer than two days, and would have blocked Hirata's train to Nagasaki. Furthermore, the epicenter of the Kobe quake was on the northern end of Awaji Island - 20 kilometers away from the city proper. The Kobe tracks were made with far sturdier and more sophisticated construction techniques and much greater repair resources were available for the job, by comparison with wartime 'just nuked' Hiroshima.

Anyway, the testimonies of Hirata, Sawachika, and Kita do seem fully consistent among themselves. They all give clear evidence for effects (damage and casualties) *within the 5 psi blast contour*. Actually, more like effects *within the 10 psi contour*. But when you put those testimonies up against actual and hypothetical blast contour maps, things get weird.

The following table 1, based on Department of Defense data from Glasstone and Dolan (1977) and Sartori (1983), summarizes the effects of increasing blast pressure on various structures and the human body. This data originates from weapons tests and blast studies to assess the effect of blast overpressure on structures and people. This data provides some guidance on the possible effects of mine explosions on miners.

Table 1 – Effect of various long duration blast overpressures and the associated maximum wind speed on various structures and the human body.

Peak overpressure	Maximum wind speed	Effect on structures	Effect on the human body
1 psi	38 mph	Window glass shatters	Light injuries from fragments occur
2 psi	70 mph	Moderate damage to houses (windows and doors blown out and severe damage to roofs)	People injured by flying glass and debris
3 psi	102 mph	Residential structures collapse	Serious injuries are common, fatalities may occur
5 psi	163 mph	Most buildings collapse	Injuries are universal, fatalities are widespread
10 psi	294 mph	Reinforced concrete buildings are severely damaged or demolished	Most people are killed
20 psi	502 mph	Heavily built concrete buildings are severely damaged or demolished	Fatalities approach 100%

PSI values with expected effects.

In order to get 5 psi effects **at the distances indicated** in the set of personal testimonies above, you would need a bomb of about 100 kilotons – more than six times the conventionally reported Little Boy yield of 15 kilotons. Actually, I'm being generous, because the height of detonation in the nuke map 100 kiloton blast overlay at Hiroshima ground zero is set to maximize the range of 5 psi effect, not the actual reported height. Furthermore, in the map shown, even the 5 psi contour extends significantly less than 4 kilometers. These generous concessions are sufficient to more than cover any worries that the damage in the testimonies was possibly characteristic of "only" 4 or 3 psi. To push the 5 psi ring out to the location of the most distant testimony would take an absurdly large yield.

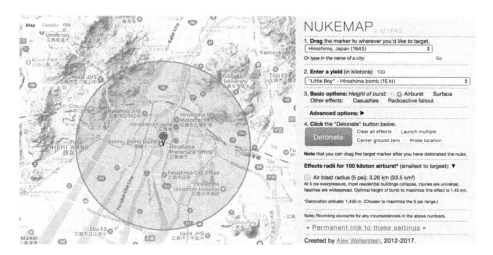

For 5 psi effects at ranges greater than 3 km from Hiroshima ground zero, you need a bomb with 100-kiloton yield – 6 times Little Boy's reported power. See Bibliography for attribution of map and overlay effect.

If there really were all these 5 psi effects that far out, at 4 kilometers or more (thus indicating a 100 kiloton yield), then what about Koi Station? Recall its location - about 2 kilometers from the hypocenter. Under this new estimate of yield, supported by the testimonies, Koi Station would have been subjected to 10 psi (or greater) effects. Yet the staff survived, the tracks were ok, and service was quickly restored.

We have a choice here. We can:

1. accept the testimonies of the moment of blast, but
2. discount any report of taking trains from Koi within two days, and also
3. massively upgrade the estimate of Little Boy's power.

Or, we can:

1. accept the train service story, and
2. retain the Little Boy yield estimate of 15 kilotons – but then

3. discount the survivor testimonies above (and a number of other similar accounts).

But the whole package together isn't self-consistent, and whichever option we go with, we will be required to discount at least a portion of Hirata's testimony. I am not, by the way, impugning Pellegrino's integrity here. He's a respected scientist and successful author with impressive Hollywood connections. Even the most scrupulous analyst can be taken in by unreliable testimony from an apparently credible witness. That could happen to any of us.

Further confirmation of these estimates of blast strength comes from official USA archives:

> *Between zero point and the main building of the novitiate of Jesuits four miles away, was a hill which served to lessen the intensity of the blast. Yet despite this protection, all the windows were shattered and part of the wall blown in. The chapel, which is the left wing of the building, is built of timber with plaster walls. The glass in the foyer windows was shattered and the roof was blown loose by the force of the explosion occurring four miles away.*
>
> ('The Atom Strikes' 1945)

Here, at **four miles distance**, we see blast effects of at least 1.5 psi, possibly greater (note the intervening hill). Those effects at that distance require the 100-kiloton bomb, just as with the other testimonies.

Medical Testimony

Professor Richard Muller (U.C. Berkeley) has stated that: "*The death from radiation and radioactivity in Hiroshima was really quite small. Mostly it was the blast.*" This seems to be borne out by interview statements from Brigadier General Crawford F. Sams (chief of Public Health and Welfare Section of the General Headquarters, Supreme Allied Powers from October 2, 1945 until June, 1951.)

Sams was not a nuclear weapons skeptic. He did assume and believe that an atomic weapon was detonated over Hiroshima. All the more reason to take his assessment of the actual situation regarding radiation sickness deaths seriously. It's interesting to sense the tension that apparently existed at the time between those who wanted to play up atomic horrors (either as a deterrent to war or as macho posturing) and those who wanted to play them down (to appear humanitarian).

> *Nothing could be established in Japan by any agency from the United States without our permission. The Manhattan Project was very interested in assessing the damage done by the atomic bomb, and so other agencies were. The Public Health Service sent over a mission, the Navy sent over people. I had a dozen different groups of medical people in, wanting to know about the effects of the atomic bomb, which was under my control. I had taken the first group down on the second of September, no, it was about the third,– into Hiroshima. I sent down six plane loads and went down to introduce some of our medical people. When I was first in Hiroshima and landed this group, I got on the radio and some professor from Columbia was saying that "anybody who got into Hiroshima in the next fifty years would die of radiation." We'd get this nonsense all the time.*
>
> *I set up, out there then, a Joint Atomic Bomb Casualty Commission. The American thing was authorized and financed from the United States – the Atomic Energy Commission – but we got the Ministry of Health and Welfare to set up a commission there and so it was jointly staffed with the Japanese. We set up a long-term project on the effects of this radiation.*
>
> *I mentioned deterrents against war. There was a letter brought over, in which the President was looking for a new deterrent against a future war, because air power had failed. You know, "If you have another war, air power will destroy civilization," and it failed because it hadn't even brought Germany to its knees. A strategic bomb survey over there showed that military production had increased actually during our bombings. So the object of Letter of Instruction, was "You will play*

up the devastating effect of the atomic bomb." I was the one who set the deadline. Anybody who had been in Hiroshima and died within six months, whether they got run over by a bicycle or whatnot, would be credited to the atomic bomb. Most of the casualties occurred from thermal readings.

The atomic bomb went off and that city had about 250 thousand people in it. In other words, you had a high density population exposed. When the bomb went off, about 2 thousand people out of 250 thousand got killed – by blast, by thermal radiation, or by intense x-ray, gamma radiation. Then, what happened is like an earthquake. The blast knocked down houses, hibachis had turned over and started fires. When you have an earthquake or an atomic bomb, you start fires and then people are trapped in the buildings. And again, by endless interviews, "Where were you?" "Where was your great uncle?" "Where was grandma when this occurred?" We built up the evidence to show on a cookie-cutter basis that it took about thirty-six hours for about two-thirds of that town to burn.

You see, it wasn't "Bing" like the publicity here [said]: a bomb went off and a city disappeared. No such thing happened. That was the propaganda for deterrent. They're talking about after that, "One bomb and away goes Chicago," you know? All you've got to do is look in Life magazine and whatnot back in '45, '46, and so on. What I'm trying to do is to show how it's like "End the war with one B-17." Well, you have to keep your feet on the ground. As near as we could figure then, about twenty-one thousand people died in thirty-six hours as a result of being trapped and burned and so on. It's like those who died in the '23 earthquake [and subsequent] fire. Then, as I say, I set the six months' deadline for anybody who had been there, even though they went away and so on, to put a deadline on deaths from delayed radiation effects.

One of us got a priest there to say he guessed 100 thousand people died when the bomb went off. Well, you see, it didn't. There never was 100 thousand people [who] died. When I came back to this country, I was appalled, from a military standpoint, to find that our major *planners in the War Department were using their own propaganda, 100 thousand deaths, Bing! And [they were] comparing it – saying it was the greatest killer in comparing it to the number of deaths in Tokyo, which had been literally destroyed by high explosives. Actually, the atomic bomb was a damn poor killer in comparison to the exposed population.*

I used to tell them back in the general staff and including the chief of staff, "If you can deter a war, for God's sake, let's do it and blow up the effects all you want. But don't believe your own propaganda if you are applying it to your military planning." Actually, the atomic bomb was a poor killer.

Fire in the Hole!

Anywhere you care to look, in the library or on the web, you'll find plentiful renditions of the Enola Gay's mission, timeline and details of the attack. I'm not going to rehash all the military procedure stuff. I'm not even going to quibble about little things, such as the post-mission buildup of bombardier Thomas W. Ferebee's supposedly preternatural skill in dropping Little Boy close to the aiming point, by pulling a switch or cord or something at just the perfect moment to earn his place in history.

In fact, after a B-29's bombardier locked onto a visually determined target at the start of a bombing run, and then making a few adjustments to insure the heading stayed straight in the face of crosswinds and other interference, the bombsight mechanism took over the plane prior to the drop. By means of the auto-pilot, the bombsight enforced its precision adjustments to the heading as needed, then automatically released the bomb at the right moment (in reality often wildly off). There was no special button or cord that needed a heroic or genius little tug at the Moment of Truth. That's all myth making. But I'm not going to get into that kind of mission trivia. I'm more interested in what supposedly happened next.

Immediately following the bomb's release, Tibbets executed his signature and much-practiced sharp diving turn away from the detonation point. Here's an account of the immediate post-detonation situation on the Enola Gay:

> Though already eleven and a half miles away, the Enola Gay was rocked by the blast. At first, Tibbets thought he was taking flak. After a second shock wave (reflected from the ground) hit the plane, the crew looked back at Hiroshima. "The city was hidden by that awful cloud... boiling up, mushrooming, terrible and incredibly tall," Tibbets recalled.
>
> (www.learnnc.org/lp/editions/nchist-worldwar/5891)

Now consider some timing details of the shock wave and the mushroom cloud formation and rise. Here's the timing on the shocks:

> Martin Harwit's 1996 book, 'An Exhibit Denied: Lobbying the History of "Enola Gay," says, "The shock wave arrived another 45 seconds later [after the detonation]," This was the direct shock wave; a few seconds later a second, ground reflected shock also hit the Enola Gay.)
>
> ('Chases and Escapes: The Mathematics of Pursuit and Evasion'
> Paul J. Nahin)

For brevity, I'm going to leave aside detailed interrogation about the occurrence of these shocks. The *Enola Gay* dove only about 2,000 feet in the escape turn, putting it at no lower than 28,000 feet, probably higher.

> At 17 seconds past 9:15 am at 30,000 feet, Col. Tibbetts dropped the bomb while Chuck Sweeney in Great Artiste dropped his instrument packages. Tibbetts immediately put Enola Gay into a hard 60 degree bank to the right, and Sweeney made the same turn to the left. When they straightened out to level flight they had lost 1,700 feet of elevation.
>
> (user.xmission.com/~tmathews/b29/155degree/155degreemath.html)

At that altitude, by that time, there should have been no separate shock of 'ground reflection' because the Mach Effect (merger) would have already occurred.

> *When an* [air burst] *occurs it sends out a shock wave like an expanding soap bubble. If the explosion occurs above the ground the bubble expands and when it reaches the ground it is reflected - i.e. the shock front bounces off the ground to form a second shock wave travelling behind the first. This second shock wave travels faster than the first, or direct, shock wave since it is travelling through air already moving at high speed due to the passage of the direct wave. The reflected shock wave tends to overtake the direct shock wave and when it does they combine to form a single reinforced wave. This is called the Mach Effect, and produces a skirt around the base of the shock wave bubble where the two shock waves have combined. This skirt sweeps outward as an expanding circle along the ground with an amplified effect compared to the single shock wave produced by a ground burst.*
>
> ('Nuclear Weapons Frequently Asked Questions' Carey Sublette)

But let's not get sidetracked by small anomalies. Eyes on the prize! Let's just carry on with the mission.

> *Enola Gay circled Hiroshima a total of three times, beginning at 29,200 feet and climbing towards 60,000 feet, before heading for home. It was 368 miles from Hiroshima before* [tailgunner] *Bob Caron reported that the mushroom cloud was no longer visible.*
>
> (Atomic Heritage Foundation)

Let's flashback to that 'circling' interval. Tibbets called for verbal descriptions from the crewmembers, beginning with the tail gunner.

Tibbets addressed the crew. "Okay. That was the reflected shock wave, bounced back from the ground. There won't be any more. It wasn't flak. Stay calm. Now, let's get these recordings going. Beser, you set?"

"Yes, Colonel."

"I want you to go around to each of the crew and record their impressions. Keep it short, and keep it clean. Bob, start talking."

"Gee, Colonel. It's just spectacular."

"Just describe what you can see. Imagine you're doing a radio broadcast."

With the Enola Gay beginning to orbit at 29,200 feet, eleven miles from Hiroshima, the tail gunner produced a vivid eyewitness account.

"A column of smoke rising fast. It has a fiery red core. A bubbling mass, purple-gray in color, with that red core. It's all turbulent. Fires are springing up everywhere, like flames shooting out of a huge bed of coals. I am starting to count the fires. One, two, three, four, five, six ... fourteen, fifteen ... it's impossible. There are too many to count. Here it comes, the mushroom shape that Captain Parsons spoke about. . . . It's like a mass of bubbling molasses. The mushroom is spreading out. It's maybe a mile or two wide and half a mile high. It's nearly level with us and climbing. It's very black, but there is a purplish tint to the cloud. The base of the mushroom looks like a heavy undercast that is shot through with flames. The city must be below that. The flames and smoke are billowing out, whirling out into the foothills. All I can see now of the city is the main dock and what looks like an airfield."

('The Bomb: A Life' Gerard DeGroot)

Caron's description has a number of interesting features:

- Pre-scripting: 'the mushroom shape that Captain Parson spoke about'
- Height: 'nearly level with us' at 'half a mile high'
- Color: 'purple-gray', 'red core', 'molasses', 'very black', 'heavy undercast'
- Visibility: 'the main dock'

Let's consider these one at a time. First, the reference to a 'mushroom shape'. This was a pre-insertion by Parsons at the mission pre-briefing.

> "No one," Parsons continued, "knows exactly what will happen when the bomb is dropped from the air. That has never been done before." He drew the shape of a mushroom on the blackboard and said: "We do expect a cloud this shape to rise at least 30,000 feet and maybe 60,000 feet, preceded by a flash of light much brighter than the sun's."
>
> ('Inferno: The Fall of Japan 1945' Ronald Henkoff)

You have to wonder whether that image would have emerged spontaneously at this moment to a truly naïve observer with no background in atomic weaponry. It sounds like pre-seeding based on the earliest bomb fiction. Those who've read detailed accounts of the *Enola Gay* mission will easily recognize the many parallels in this 1914 science fiction:

> *The sky above the indistinct horizons of this cloud sea was at first starry and then paler with a light that crept from north to east as the dawn came on. The Milky Way was invisible in the blue, and the lesser stars vanished. The face of the adventurer at the steering-wheel, darkly visible ever and again by the oval greenish glow of the compass face, had something of that firm beauty which all concentrated purpose gives, and something of the happiness of an idiot child that has at last got hold of the matches. His companion, a less imaginative type, sat with his legs spread wide over the long, coffin-shaped box which contained in its compartments the three atomic bombs, the new bombs that would continue to explode indefinitely and which no one so far had ever seen in action.*
>
> *Hitherto Carolinum, their essential substance, had been tested only in almost infinitesimal quantities within steel chambers embedded in lead. Beyond the thought of great destruction slumbering in the black spheres between his legs, and a keen resolve to follow out very exactly the instructions that had been given him, the man's mind was a blank.*

His aquiline profile against the starlight expressed nothing but a profound gloom.. The sky below grew clearer as the Central European capital was approached... So far they had been singularly lucky and had been challenged by no aeroplanes at all. The frontier scouts they must have passed in the night; probably these were mostly under the clouds; the world was wide and they had had luck in not coming close to any soaring sentinel. Their machine was painted a pale gray, that lay almost invisibly over the cloud levels below. But now the east was flushing with the near ascent of the sun, Berlin was but a score of miles ahead, and the luck of the Frenchmen held. By imperceptible degrees the clouds below dissolved.... Sure of its accessibility, he craned his neck over the side of the aeroplane and judged his pace and distance. Then very quickly he bent forward, bit the stud, and hoisted the bomb over the side. 'Round,' he whispered inaudibly. ... The bomb flashed blinding scarlet in mid-air, and fell, a descending column of blaze eddying spirally in the midst of a whirlwind. Both the aeroplanes were tossed like shuttlecocks, hurled high and sideways and the steersman, with gleaming eyes and set teeth, fought in great banking curves for a balance. The gaunt man clung tight with hand and knees; his nostrils dilated, his teeth biting his lips. He was firmly strapped.... When he could look down again it was like looking down upon the crater of a small volcano. In the open garden before the Imperial castle a shuddering star of evil splendour spurted and poured up smoke and flame towards them like an accusation. They were too high to distinguish people clearly, or mark the bomb's effect upon the building until suddenly the facade tottered and crumbled before the flare as sugar dissolves in water.

('The World Set Free' H. G. Wells 1914)

But I digress. Most importantly, consider the height estimate of the developing cloud. Here we find something extremely odd. By hypothesis and every account, at this stage the Enola Gay was circling at minimum 29,000 feet. The cloud is said to be 'level with us'. Yet at the same time, the cloud is estimated to be 'half a mile high' (2,640 feet). All sources seem to agree that these mushroom clouds rise up very quickly. 'The Effects of Nuclear Weapons', a federal guide, informs us that nuclear mushroom clouds typically reach their maximum heights in about 10 minutes. Based on estimates from other sources, the Little Boy cloud would have risen to over 60,000 feet in about that time.

So there is the *Enola Gay*, post-detonation, post-shock wave (#1), post-shock wave (#2), safely circling and climbing. Then, there was the time taken for reassurance from Captain Tibbets and for his instructions, and now the tail gunner is talking. We've seen that the shock waves could not have finished much earlier than one minute, and we should allow at least another couple minutes for the other activities listed above.

Let's make a conservative simplifying assumption that the hypothetical mushroom cloud has at that point had three minutes and twenty seconds to develop. We can't assume strict linearity for the cloud's rise over time, but at least, if it's non-linear, the early phase is the more likely to be hyperlinear. So let's be conservative again and call those first three minutes at least linear, in the absence of any better information. So that's one third of our ten minutes, to get one third of our 60,000-foot final height, thus the cloud was at 20,000 feet. How is that 'level with us' at 29,000 feet? Most crucially, how is that, at the same time, 'half a mile high'? Somebody screwed up the scripting there.

As for color, the cloud is described in no uncertain terms as basically dark. Remember that the description we're concerned with here realistically could not have been earlier than after three full minutes of development. Here is a photo said to be of the Little Boy mushroom cloud. How dark is that?

Death Object

White (putative) mushroom cloud of Hiroshima

It's interesting that Caron mentions the dock area's visibility, because there's a final fatal gotcha on this Enola Gay urban legend. On that morning, by chance an unauthorized B-29 had somehow missed the word banning all non-mission flights to or near Hiroshima that morning. This was a reconnaissance plane whose crew included photographer John McGlohon. According to newspaper accounts, it has now been verified that *"the photos [McGlohon] took minutes after the explosion were the only ones made looking straight down on Hiroshima as the mushroom cloud was enveloping it."*

> *McGlohon's plane, piloted by Jack Economos, left in the early hours of Aug. 6 for a long flying day, to photograph potential targets near Hiroshima, Kure and farther north. As they neared Hiroshima around 8:15 a.m., a gunner reported over the intercom seeing a B-29 flying in the opposite direction as if headed for an emergency landing at Iwo Jima. Often, McGlohon says, when bombers had engine trouble, they would abort their missions, drop their bomb loads and try to reach a friendly landing site. Within seconds, McGlohon said, "There was a brilliant flash below our plane. The light was as if someone had fired a big flashbulb directly in your eyes." "We assumed the bomber had salvoed his bomb load and managed to get a good hit on an ammunition dump or an oil tank, so the day wouldn't be a total loss," McGlohon said. He turned on his cameras to shoot the damage and the cloud that was rising from below so that later, "The crew could get credit for the good job they had done."*
>
> (www.mcclatchydc.com)

There's a big tortuous saga of how his film later got mixed up and lost or suppressed for decades, and how his account of being on the scene was doubted and denied but eventually verified. For our purposes, what matters is the photo he supposedly shot from directly above the city.

Death Object

This is said to be the only known photo looking straight down on Hiroshima immediately after the atomic bomb was dropped.

This photo was shot after McGlohon's plane had flown toward and over the city, passing the Enola Gay on its way out. McGlohon wanted to take some photos as soon as he realized something was blowing up under their plane. Here's an account of his plane's timing and location:

> *At the moment the bomb exploded, McGlohon and his crew were approaching Hiroshima at about 27,000 feet and flying at least 275 mph. They would have passed over the city before the mushroom cloud had time to reach their altitude.*
>
> ('Scars of War' Marilyn Swinson)

If McGlohon was able to be directly over Hiroshima after the detonation yet before the mushroom cloud had developed sufficiently to alarm or block him (or even be noticed by him as such), his plane would have been destroyed by the shock wave(s). Recall from the prior discussion that the mushroom cloud boiled up to 20,000 feet within one minute of detonation. Remember that *Enola Gay* felt two big shocks, described by Tibbets: *"We were eleven and a half miles slant range from the atomic explosion, but the whole plane cracked and crinkled from the blast."* That was at 45 seconds after detonation, as we've seen. Now consider McGlohon's plane: it is described as being 'directly above' a mushroom cloud that had to have been already 20,000 feet high or more, as we've already seen.

But since McGlohon certainly wasn't directly on top of the Enola Gay when the bomb was dropped, it had to be that his plane flew straight into a hugely rising, roiling mushroom cloud, of at least 20,000 feet height, without noticing anything special, and focusing only on the 'good job' somebody had done far below, hitting 'an ammo dump or an oil tank'.

Since McGlohon's plane was neither swatted from the sky by the shock waves (if he was above the drop point between detonation and mushroom cloud rising) and given that he doesn't seem to have flown straight into or around an amazing 20,000+ foot mushroom cloud, clearly his straight-down overhead photo is not of the mushroom cloud – at any stage. Nor could it have been the mature Hiroshima firestorm, which just after the strike had barely begun to develop.

It's obvious that here we have an overhead photo of a firestorm in Hiroshima, without any nuke shock waves or mushroom cloud involved. How do you get a firestorm without a nuclear explosion? You do it with a garden-variety incendiaries-plus-high-explosives saturation raid. McGlohon's picture, which he seems to have shot in good faith, shows Hiroshima in the early (or early-to-mid) phase of an 'ordinary' firestorm caused by a normal-for-the-times firebombing. The kind of raid the 20th Air Group performed, with factory-like precision and saturation coverage, *all throughout 1945*. Notice how the smoke contour ends just before the water line. There's no reason for a nuclear cloud to respect the water line (do keep in mind that this was supposedly shot well before any nuclear-triggered firestorm could have kicked in).

But, wind factors apart, firestorms from incendiary bombing do respect the water line, at least for a while. Compare this photo of a slightly earlier stage of a standard fire-bombing. What we see below is a similar white incendiary smoke cover beginning to fill the space up to the water line and docks.

Incendiary bombing of Kobe in-progress.

Fool Me Twice: Japan 1945

Tarumiza firebombing and start of smoke cover.

The reason for the McGlohon's unauthorized presence in the area is explained as follows:

> *Before the bombing, an order was issued to the 20th Air Force barring its planes from flying within 50 miles of Hiroshima the morning of August 6. McGlohon's unit was not on the distribution list* [for this order].

('Scars of War' Marilyn Swinson)

It's natural to suppose that an order to keep extraneous units out was motivated by concerns about interference with the singular atomic mission, for the safety of uninvolved planes, and for general high-security. But it may be that the order was not intended to keep the skies safe, it was to keep the real operation secret. They needed a decent-size formation to do the fire-bombing. It's more likely the order was to keep the skies clear *of anybody without a need to know*.

Death Object

If there had been a full sequence of professionally executed surveillance photos from *Necessary Evil*, the mission's photography plane, none of this sleuthing would be necessary. Everything would be cleared up instantly. But no complete, clear, time-stamped and geo-located output from *Necessary Evil*'s assigned mission seems to be available.

Matsushige Photographs

For on-site ground-level documentation, we have the small photo archive created by Matsushige Yoshito (松重 美人) on the day.

> On August 6, 1945, Yoshito Matsushige was 32 years old, living at home in Midori-cho, Hiroshima. His home was 1.7 miles away from ground zero, just outside of the 1.5 mile radius of the total destruction created by atomic blast effects. Miraculously, Matsushige was not seriously injured by the explosion. With one camera and two rolls of film with 24 possible exposures, he tried to photograph the immediate aftereffects of the bombing of Hiroshima.
>
> (Atomic Heritage Foundation)

He described his actions that day as follows:

> *I had finished breakfast and was getting ready to go to the newspaper when it happened. There was a flash from the indoor wires as if lightening had struck. I didn't hear any sound, how shall I say, the world around me turned bright white. And I was momentarily blinded as if a magnesium light had lit up in front of my eyes. Immediately after that, the blast came. I was bare from the waist up, and the blast was so intense, it felt like hundreds of needles were stabling me all at once. The blast grew large holes in the walls of the first and second floor. I could barely see the room because of all the dirt. I pulled my camera and the clothes issued by the military headquarters out from under the mound of the debris, and I got dressed. I thought I would go to either the newspaper or to the headquarters. That was about 40 minutes after the blast.*
>
> (Matsushige Yoshito)

From this account, given the ambiguity in his statement that he'd go to "*either the newspaper or to the headquarters*", it seems most probable that he was saying he *set out* from his house at 40 minutes after the blast, rather than that he *arrived* at either of those destinations at 40 minutes after the blast. In fact, it's not clear from the rest of his account that he ever arrived at either location on that day, which further reinforces the departure time interpretation that I'm adopting.

Clearly he was not in a position to photograph the immediate blast. He took five famous street-level photos. They are close up or mid-distance shots of survivors, rescuers and damage. His camera was a Kodak Retina, a popular small walk-about camera of the 1930's, not equipped with telephoto lens or zoom capability. (It appears that the Kilfitt 3682 mm/2.8 Zoomar introduced in 1959 was the first varifocal lens in regular production for still 35mm photography.) I mention Matsushige Yoshito because he is often wrongly credited with a shot more relevant to my analysis.

Death Object

 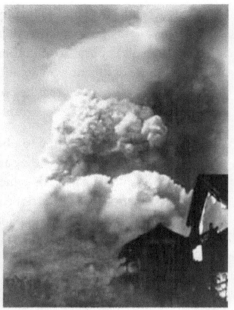

The early Hiroshima mushroom cloud? Often mis-attributed to Matsushige Yoshito.

This photograph, purporting to show the early Little Boy mushroom cloud, should be credited to a *different* photographer with the *same* surname: Matsushige Tatuso (松重三男). It is correctly attributed in the 2-panel version reproduced here. All that seems to be known about him is the following:

> Mitsuo Matsushige was at home in Furuichi-cho, in the outskirts of Hiroshima, when the atomic bomb exploded. When he saw the flash, he dashed outside and witnessed the orange fireball rise rapidly in the sky leaving a trail. Three days later, he went to his workplace in Fukuromachi, 500 meters from the hypocenter, and found the entire area a burnt plain.

The two-panel illustration shows a single photograph. On the left side, the contrast and sharpness are retained from the original negative. On the right side, the contrast and sharpness have been muted in order to eliminate the flames, sparks, and embers rising from below. On Japanese websites, the two versions are sometimes contrasted as evidence of censorship of aspects of the event. As for timing, this is variously said to be "immediately following" or "2 minutes after" the detonation.

For our purposes, we only need to note the attributed distance of 7 kilometers (4.3 miles). You needn't be a whacko conspiracy theorist to find something odd about this picture as described, if it's meant to show the mushroom cloud formation. This photographer was able to rush outside, with his camera, and capture a very close-up shot, without a zoom lens, of a fireball rising 4 miles away, with the fire having apparently already reached his own neighborhood. If this is the start of the mushroom cloud, the top is way low. Even at 2 minutes post-detonation, by our previous analysis, the top should have been much higher. If the shot was taken at that early time, from as close as it appears (no zoom lens), then the blast (not just ground flames) should have affected the cameraman and surroundings. In short, this photographer was not 4 miles from the billow he's photographing, and if all these things (camera position, house, mushroom billow) are as close together as they appear, everything should have been blown to spit.

It likely that this is actually a photo of a close incendiary strike, a ground level view of something like one of the incendiary hits on Yokohama.

Death Object

Incendiary raid smoke billows at Yokohama.

No Bald Spot

Apart from any other nitpicking and anomaly chasing, the key deal breaker for the orthodox story of atomic Hiroshima is the fact that there was no 'bald spot'. The damage was uniform to the perimeters, exactly as in a typical firebombing raid.

Tokyo. Typical firestorm damage, extensive burnout of light and wooden construction, retention of stronger or concrete structures, no central 'bald spot'. Note also the many intact bridges – similar to Hiroshima, where only one of the city's 20 bridges was disabled or destroyed (apparently collapsed by mobs fleeing fires).

What do I mean by a bald spot? When massive firepower is centered on a main central area, I want to see a serious, concentric glass parking lot (in case of nuke, glowing green). I want to see a focus area melted to sludge and slag at ground zero (immediately below air zero).

DEATH OBJECT

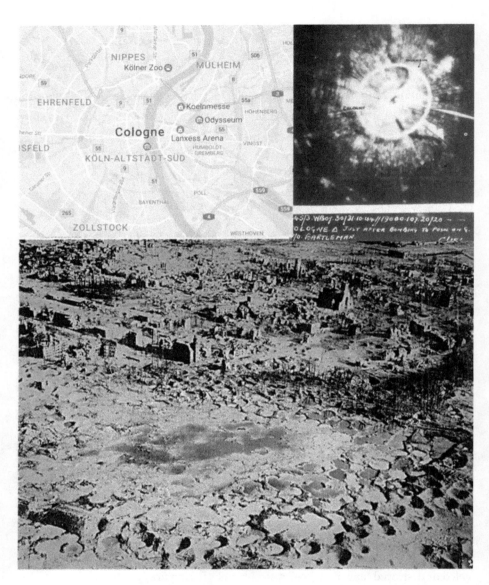

Cologne, Germany showing 'bald at center of normal fire and blast damage. Overall extent of destruction approximately equal to the map in upper left, aerial photo has 'Mulheim' hand-labeled with arrow on outer ring, and 'Cologne' written left-center.

Some interesting 'before and after' aerial collage photos of Hiroshima were made in mid-1945.

FOOL ME TWICE: JAPAN 1945

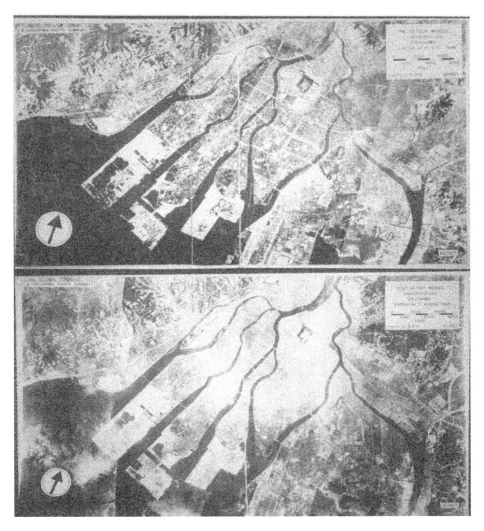

Top panel is April, bottom panel is mid-August.

There are problems all over this contrastive display. The basic function of the assembly is to draw your eyes to the center whited-out area and hit you in the gut with this kind of vibe: *"Look on my works, ye Mighty, and Weep!"* Total vaporization, devastation, glass parking lot.

But these pictures could easily be flipped and make the same point. By fiddling with the lighting, contrast, shadows, and focus knobs in Photoshop, I could interchange these photos with the same impact. You also have to wonder why are these photos assembled by strips? Though there is cloud cover in Japan, the POV is not that high off the ground. The US was bombing all cities at will. General Cutis LeMay, who ran the whole show, later said about Japan: "throughout the war, not one of our attacks was ever turned back by enemy action." *That* is what's called 'air superiority'. You wouldn't think it so difficult to get a single bird's eye view.

But using assembled strips makes it easier to play with the exposures to get the impact you want in different local zones. A few things were overlooked however. The basic theme here is: 'white = bad' i.e. anywhere that's whited out is supposed to punch our 'glass parking lot' emotional buttons. Examine then the lower left quadrant of the two pictures. That's the dock and wharves area of the port. In that zone, the after picture looks more devastated than the before shot (using the white-out criteria that we're intended to apply to the hypocenter near the top-center area). All good you say? But wait: neither the blast nor the fire ever reached nearly that far.

Fool Me Twice: Japan 1945

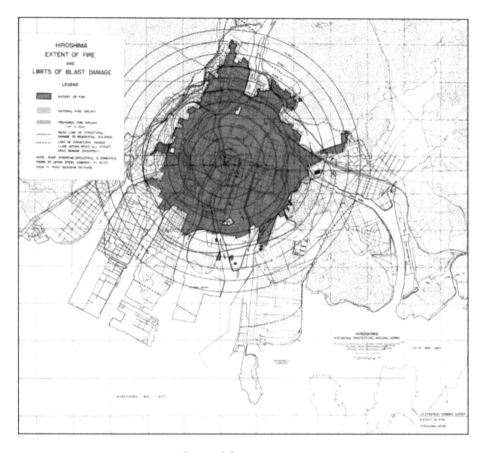

Blast and fire extent map.

Conversely, look at the lower right quadrant. Here, if the degree of white-out is our criteria, we have the opposite problem: in that area, the before picture is more 'devastated' than the after. It's obvious that the entire display is a carelessly tricked up piece of 'drive-by evidence', created by fiddling with strip exposures, without much attention to logic or the fire/blast map. Hiroshima was indeed wiped out. No argument there. *Both pictures* show extensive destruction (and clearance) all over the area It makes sense given the plentitude of military targets. If the whiteout in parts of both photos means anything all, it may just indicate a more advanced stage of deliberate clearance of blacker, older charred rubble – which takes time. In any case, the second was taken at a later date, but they've been synchronized in tandem; both of them tweaked and tuned to the storyline. Back in 1945, it probably took a full-day darkroom shift to trick this out, while with current digital tools it would take about 20 minutes.

Trickery is the Way of War

***Un*-Damaged or *Pre*-Damaged?**

Now we need to back up and look at what probably really happened. To do that, we need to first consider the whole *target selection* thing. It's well known that certain areas were off limits to everybody. Both LeMay's firebombing raids and the upcoming possible nuclear attacks were prohibited for Kyoto and the Imperial Palace in Tokyo. There's a whole huge history on the Kyoto thing and Secretary of War Stimson's top-down imposition of hands-off that ancient cultural city. I'm not going to go over all that. I'll just accept for purposes of this discussion that Kyoto was sidelined from the start. Likewise, there were strategic and political issues in deciding whether to target the Imperial Palace that I won't get into.

By early-to-mid 1945, what did that leave? In the documentary movie *The Fog of War*, a list of 67 Japanese cities that were, on average, 50% destroyed (usually a lot more) is scrolled out, with the percentage destruction figure for each. Hiroshima and Nagasaki were excluded from that list (in the documentary's otherwise unrelated storyline), obviously understood as special cases. Those two *were* especially useful cases – but not perhaps in the way usually thought.

Up to late spring of 1945, the United States strategic bombing and carrier forces had already engaged in continuous attacks of relentless ferocity against the 67 cities – many of which were of far lesser size and military significance than Hiroshima. Here is the attitude of the field commanders up to the end of Spring 1945 and probably much later:

> [The] *Joint Staff* [reported] *in April 1945 that our course should be:*
> *Apply full and unremitting pressure against Japan by strategic bombing and carrier raids in order to reduce war-making capability and to demoralize the country in preparation for invasion*
> ('Now It Can be Told' Leslie Groves)

No mention whatsoever of an amazing new super weapon. The field commanders had no real awareness of the progress of the atomic bomb project, no conception of its potential strategic utility and no plan for its incorporation in real war fighting. They focused entirely on their vision of *"no stone left atop another"*. Given that by April 1945, they had bombed out over 60% of numerous relatively minor strategic sites (the 67 mentioned above), is it likely that Hiroshima had truly been left pristine? It comes down to a question of military value: did Hiroshima have any?

> Hiroshima [was] *a major port of embarkation for the Japanese Army and a convoy assembly point for their Navy. The city, in which the local Army headquarters, with some twenty-five thousand troops, was situated, was mainly concentrated on four islands. The railway yards, Army storage depots and port of embarkation lay along the eastern side of the city. A number of heavy industrial facilities were adjacent to the main metropolitan area.*
>
> (Leslie Groves)

Hmm. Keep in mind that up to early summer of 1945, there was no atomic target list of 'reserved cities'. That happened later, after secret committees had been formed in Washington D.C. and wide-ranging discussions had been held:

> *At about this time, the Spring of 1945, another job was dropped into our laps at the* [Manhattan Engineering District]. *The first inkling I had of this added responsibility came in the course of a conversation with General Marshall. We had been discussing the progress of the work, and, having mentioned our anticipated readiness date, I suggested that the time was fast approaching when we should begin to make plans for the bombing operation itself, even though we still had no assurance that the bomb would be effective. I asked him to designate some officer in the Operations Planning Division (OPD) of the General Staff with whom I could liaison with whom I could get in touch so that planning could be started. After a moment's hesitation,*

> General Marshall replied: "I don't like to bring too many people into this matter. Is there any reason why you can't take this over and do it yourself?" My "No, sir, I will" concluded the conversation, which constituted the only directive that I ever received or needed.
>
> (Leslie Groves)

Before Groves could create the target list (and thus, the reserved or protected list), he had to consider many factors:

> I had set as the governing factor that the targets chosen should be places the bombing of which would most adversely affect the will of the Japanese people to continue the war. Beyond that, they should be military in nature, consisting either of important headquarters or troop concentrations, or centers of production of military equipment and supplies. To accurately assess the effects of the bomb, the targets should not have been previously damaged by air raids. It was also desirable that the first target be of such size that the damage would be confined within it, so that we could more definitely determine the power of the bomb.
>
> (Leslie Groves)

Here is our first mention of the 'undamaged' criterion. Again, we see emphasis on the strategic/military value of Hiroshima – obvious to General Groves even at his remove of thousands of miles from the battlespace. The 'reserved' list was the output of a committee that Groves then set up:

> The next step was to set up a special committee to recommend specific targets. This group met for the first time on May 2 in Washington.
>
> At its third meeting, the Target Committee was informed that General Arnold and I had concluded that control over the use of the weapon should reside, for the present, in Washington. This announcement was necessary because some of the Air Force people on the committee had

displayed a total lack of comprehension of what was involved. The operation would not be formally considered and acted upon by either the Joint Chiefs of Staff or the Combined Chiefs. One of the reasons for this was the need to maintain complete security. Equally important though, was Admiral Leahy's disbelief in the weapon and its hoped-for effectiveness; this would have made action by the Joint Chiefs quite difficult. When our target cities were first selected, an order was sent to the Army Air Force in Guam not to bomb them without special authority from the War Department.

(Leslie Groves)

So now finally, no earlier than May 1945, we get the first order to the field concerning what was to be 'reserved' and 'protected'. It's most likely that Hiroshima (and Nagasaki as we'll see) was not chosen as an A-bomb because it was *'un-*damaged' – rather, it was chosen because it was *'pre-*damaged – in just the right way to serve as the movie set for an atomic attack of the type that had been advertised to the brass as the Manhattan Project payday.

Reconnaissance revealed to the Committee that Hiroshima had been pre-pounded in such a way that the destruction could, with perhaps a pre-dawn finalizing raid and some dog-and-pony psyop work, be represented as a city that had gone from fully populated, undamaged normal functioning to a total moonscape in less than 60 seconds. It was apparently the best choice among the 67 pre-damaged alternatives they must have considered. After the war, the records would have been scrubbed to make it appear that Hiroshima had, *by some kind of telepathic precognition,* been mysteriously spared or 'pre-reserved' – throughout half of 1943, all of 1944, and half of 1945 - by the otherwise incessantly bloodthirsty and hyper-active United States strategic bombing command.

But, for the sake of argument, let's stick with the standard story. Let's assume that for some unfathomable reason, the Hiroshima core city area had not, as of August 5th, been raided and burned out. Let's take Hiroshima as the one remaining unblemished plum, or at least as a pre-damaged target that still required some finishing touches and some final tenderizing. It's well established that on the night prior to the Enola Gay mission, a big operation went out:

> *To divert attention, a major effort by the 20th AF was conducted on the night of 5/6 August 1945 by 602 B-29's striking a variety of targets including the urban areas of: Saga, Maebaski, Nishinomiya, Imabari, the oil refinery at Ube and various mining targets. The biggest effort by 250 planes was against Nishinomiya, a town close to the Inland Sea and about 140 miles east of Hiroshima. This effort was in lieu of the initial request by the Corps of Engineers to Gen. LeMay for 1000 B-29's to accompany the atomic bomb to the Empire.*
>
> ('No Strategic Targets Left' F. J. Bradley)

Got that? They had the capability of sending 1000 B-29's out to accompany the 'special mission' – but supposedly they did not. A few targets are listed above, but the word 'including' indicates that list is not exhaustive. Contemporary news stories in US newspapers confirmed that there was a "*580-plane attack in the pre-dawn of Aug. 6 with 3,840 tons of bombs on four cities and a coal liquefaction plant.*" Some of these target cities are very close to Hiroshima.

> *During the night of August 5–6, Japanese early warning radar detected the approach of numerous American aircraft headed for the southern part of Japan. Radar detected 65 bombers headed for Saga, 102 bound for Maebashi, 261 en route to Nishinomiya, 111 headed for Ube and 66 bound for Imabari.*
>
> (Wikipedia)

Most of those target cities had already been bombed to useless, scantily populated junkyards months prior. The drive-by rationale is usually offered (as in the account above) that the August raids were just a 'diversionary' tactic. And yet, by this time the USA had absolute air superiority over Japan and could operate from the air with impunity. So I can't help wondering – diverting *whose* attention from *what*, exactly?

From the above account, we know that Imabari was supposedly targeted that night. It's possible that Kure, a major (already destroyed) naval base near Hiroshima, may have been specified as another so-called 'diversionary' target.

Fool Me Twice: Japan 1945

In general the Hiroshima neighborhood was a target-rich area, as long as you didn't question why the rubble was being bounced and re-bounced. The relevant distances are shown in the map.

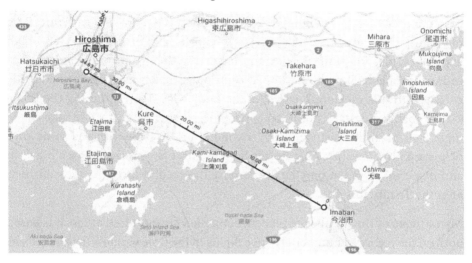

Hiroshima area targets such as Imbari (right end of distance line) and Kure (middle of distance line) separated by short air-mile flights.

There are only a few dozen air miles between Imabari and Hiroshima, with Kure along the way. As for the actual condition of Imabari at that time, dig if you will the picture:

> "When I was looking at the train timetable, I found that no trains stopped at Imabari station ... I wondered why the third largest city in the province had no train service. It sounded ridiculous... The other guy said, "Wow! No Imabari Station. But ... all the trains pass by Imabari Station." A third guy stepped up ... "It's not strange at all. There's no stop because there's no Imabari City anymore. It got burned up last April in the air raid ... No buildings, no houses, no people ... The whole city burned up and the people ran away ..." A fellow soldier explained to Manabe. "The air raids came on the 26th of April and the 8th of May. Imabari was burned up. My father was in business there. We had a wholesale draper business. All gone. All burned up."
>
>   ('Inferno: the Firebombing of Japan' Edwin Hoyt)

DEATH OBJECT

So, to summarize the Hiroshima operation, here's what likely went down.

It appears that anywhere from 250 to 1000 B-29's (exact count uncertain, depending on how much of a touch-up and light-show was needed) hit Hiroshima-area targets, including the city itself, on the night and early morning of August 5 and 6. Those attacks were the usual mix of incendiary and high explosives, blasting stuff to ruins and triggering the firestorm. Standard procedure. Probably Hiroshima proper, central districts, was hit last, to coincide closely with that morning's arrival of the Enola Gay. I am assuming the Enola Gay probably did really put in an appearance over the city, for the sake of the flight logs, posterity, history, or Hollywood. They probably released some kind of 'pumpkin' device (practice atomic bomb shell) that was rigged for a big flash and dispersal of radiation (thus becoming the second dirty bomb in history, after the Trinity 100-Ton test).

My estimate of the number of planes required, a few hundred at most, is based both on the recorded number of active flights in the time window (as we've seen) and also on the Survey's estimate of what would have been needed. Note however, that a lot of the damage was probably inflicted over the preceding several months.

> On the basis of the known destructiveness of various bombs computed from the war in Europe and the Pacific and from tests, the Survey has estimated the striking force that would have been necessary to achieve the same destruction at Hiroshima and Nagasaki. To cause physical damage equivalent to that caused by the atomic bombs, approximately 1,300 tons of bombs (one-fourth high explosives and three-fourth incendiary) would have been required at Nagasaki–in the target area. To place that many bombs in the target area, assuming daylight attacks under essentially the same conditions of weather and enemy opposition that prevailed when the atomic bombs were dropped, it is estimated that 1,600 tons of bombs would have had to be dropped at Hiroshima and 900 tons at Nagasaki. To these bomb loads would have to be added a number of tons of antipersonnel fragmentation bombs to inflict comparable casualties. These would add about 500 tons at Hiroshima and 300 tons at Nagasaki. The total bomb loads would thus

be 2,100 tons at Hiroshima (400 HE, 1,200 IB) and 1,200 tons (675 HE, 225 IB) at Nagasaki. With each plane carrying 10 tons, the attacking force required would have been 210 B-29s at Hiroshima and 120 B-29s at Nagasaki.

(U.S. Strategic Bombing Survey)

In the context of 1945 Japan strategic operations, the resource requirement for these operations is absolutely trivial. After the war, Curtis LeMay said that in the new era of the A-bomb: "one airplane does the work of hundreds". But as with any mathematical equation, it can also be reversed as needed for special operations: "Hundreds do the work of one."

Flash

Ground witnesses often mentioned the *pika-don* (ピカドン) effect. This means basically 'flash-bang'. In the chaos and madness of an incendiary raid, which includes high explosives, flashes and bangs are certainly expected. As for the single *pika* (flash) it's possible (though not really essential) that Enola Gay or another plane deployed a *photoflash* bomb.

> A photoflash bomb, or flash bomb, is explosive ordnance dropped by aircraft, usually military surveillance aircraft, designed to detonate above ground to create an extremely bright flash of light. These bombs, which are capable of producing light at an intensity of up to hundreds of millions of candlepower, assist surveillance aircraft in taking night-time aerial photos without the need to fly low to the ground which would make it vulnerable to possible enemy detection.

(Wikipedia)

Even if these were detonated at daybreak (rather than the intended night usage) anybody looking directly at the flash would feel it, just as you'd feel it if a flash camera went off in your face. It need not have been 'bright as a thousand suns' to be noticeable. One thing you sometimes hear as one of the abstractly cited effects of a nuclear bomb's flash is genuine permanent blindness. There don't seem to be very many (or any) verified cases of that, but the M46 photoflash bomb was definitely no fun to look at:

The resulting flash of light lasted for about 1/5th of a second and had a peak intensity of approximately 500,000,000 candlepower.

(www.harringtonmuseum.org.uk/m46-photoflash-bomb/)

Radiation

To those on the wrong end of the gun, 'dirty bomb' radioactive materials dispersal is not the same thing as direct exposure to atomic radiation effects. By my FAIL hypothesis, there shouldn't have been any so-called 'prompt' radiation effects from the Little Boy attack. There should be only dirty bomb types of contamination (and not a whole lot of that). Therefore, the acute radiation sickness reports must have been either misunderstood burn effects, or plain over-reporting, exaggeration and fakery. It's possible the dispersed radioactive material from Enola Gay did have an effect on some people's health, but that was not likely to have been as intense or immediate as later reported. Dirty bombs just aren't that dangerous, it's more of a psy-op concept.

Even if a real 'Little Boy' had detonated, even if everything had been strictly-to-spec by the conventional book, we should remember that the blast height and other aspects of the plan were, according to Leslie Groves, designed to *minimize radiation effects*. Even the humid air of the Japanese summer would have militated against the extreme radiation effects that were later reported. So at a minimum there must have been exaggeration of at least that aspect of the bomb effects. Please don't think I'm callous about any of this. My breezy tone just soothes the horror of having to write about such things at all. If even one person was hurt in any of this, whether s/he was carbonized, vaporized, barbecued or liquefied, that's one too many.

Moving on from the relatively straight-forward case of Hiroshima, and turning to Nagasaki, again there's the 'nuclear target list' thing. This was the short list of good nuclear attack targets that was circulating among committees and principals of the war command and the Manhattan Project.

It should be remembered that in our selection of target, the 20th Air Force is operating primarily to laying waste all the main Japanese cities, and that they do not propose to save some important primary target for us if it interferes with the operation of the war from their point of view. Their existing procedure has been to bomb the hell our of Tokyo, bomb the aircraft manufacturing and assembly, engine plants and in general paralyze the aircraft industry so as to eliminate opposition to the 20th Air Force operations. The 20th Air Force is systemically bombing out the following cities with the prime purpose in mind of not leaving one stone lying on another:

Tokyo, Yokohama, Nagoya, Osaka, Kyoto, Kobe, Yawata, & Nagasaki.

(Notes on Initial Meeting of Target Committee, May 1945)

Again, we see Nagasaki, but not Hiroshima, among the cities explicitly listed as undergoing massive destruction. That fits with the revised story of the Hiroshima 'special mission' given above.

Although only eight cities are given as examples of 'not leaving one stone lying on another', we know from the citation of 67 destroyed cities that in fact there was a lot more destruction going on at the time. So if we leave aside Kyoto and the Imperial Palace for the reasons mentioned earlier, the key elements remaining by summer of 1945 boiled down pretty much to the following choices that were to be "reserved" for the 'special missions' (atomic attacks) – Hiroshima, Kokura, Niigata.

Furthermore it confirms that Nagasaki was never on any nuclear 'reserved' list (hands off, 20th Air Force!) until days before the attack, if then. This is well-documented.

On July 24th, I send a memorandum to General Marshall at Potsdam to obtain his final approval of our plan of operation. Attached to it [was] … a one-page draft of a necessary action by the Joint Chiefs releasing the previously reserved targets (all but Nagasaki, which had never been reserved) to the Commanding General, Army Air Forces, for attack only by the 509th Group, 20th Air Force.

(Leslie Groves 'Now it Can Be Told')

Nagasaki is a long, thin city strung through a valley leading down from the north to a southern port area that gives into the sea. The southernmost part of the city is a historical and cultural hotspot. During the war, the more northerly part of the city, in and around the Urakami Valley, was the site of important arms plants and facilities. Consider this account of the result of the 'nuclear' attack on that area:

> The Fat Man weapon, containing a core of about 6.4 kg (14 lb) of plutonium, was dropped over the city's industrial valley at 32.77372°N 129.86325°E. It exploded 47 seconds later at 1,650 ± 33 ft (503 ± 10 m), above a tennis court halfway between the Mitsubishi Steel and Arms Works in the south and the Nagasaki Arsenal in the north. The radius of total destruction was about 1 mi (1.6 km), followed by fires across the northern portion of the city to 2 mi (3.2 km) south of the bomb. About 58% of the Mitsubishi Arms Plant was damaged, and about 78% of the Mitsubishi Steel Works. The Mitsubishi Electric Works suffered only 10% structural damage as it was on the border of the main destruction zone. The Nagasaki Arsenal was destroyed in the blast.
>
> (Wikipedia)

In other words, the part of Nagasaki supposedly hit by the bomb was a sweet and juicy *military target*. Yet by all accounts, it was only the purest accident of a lucky cloud break that pushed the Nagasaki atomic attack to target this plum, after diversion from Kokura due to visibility issues. Followed by diversion yet again of the drop point within Nagasaki, modified away from the (supposedly) pre-assigned aiming point which was more southerly, closer to the port area.

Let's think about how likely it was that this area would have been spared from the bombing campaign that had been raging for at least the prior year. Was this prime military zone really left untouched? Consider that for the previous 12 months or more, USA marines, sailors and airmen had been dying by the thousands, up against Japanese arms, planes, ships, bombs and torpedoes. The slogan *'Remember Pearl Harbor'* was the emotional gas tank of all that struggle and passion.

Fool Me Twice: Japan 1945

Remember Pearl Harbor

Now consider this conventional claim of one result of Fat Man over Nagasaki:

> *The Mitsubishi-Urakami Ordnance Works, the factory that manufactured the type 91 torpedoes released in the attack on Pearl Harbor, was destroyed in the blast.*
>
> (Wikipedia)

How likely is it that this factory had been spared? Especially since we *know* (see above documentation) that Nagasaki *was in fact bombed* prior to August. So

Nagasaki, far from being untouched nuclear-virgin real estate, was likely totally bombed out long before. And based on the description and logic above, most especially the military works of the Urakami Valley would have been targeted all along. Some may argue that this area would have been spared, because threaded among the arms plants were hospitals, schools, and churches. To that I say - *please*. This campaign was under the direction of General Curtis LeMay. If you tell me that Curtis LeMay spared *anything* on humanitarian grounds, I can only reply with Michael Corleone's classic comeback: *"Now who's being naïve?"*

The Urakami Valley had already been totally demolished days, weeks, or even months prior to August 1945. That state of ready-made desolation, far from ruling out Nagasaki as a nuclear target, is *precisely what most perfectly qualified the Urakami Valley for the staging of a fake attack*. Let's confirm this supposition with a closer look at the situation on the ground.

Nagasaki

Entire books have been written about the Fat Man mission, how screwed up it was (at least, relative to the picture-perfect Little Boy delivery), how Bock's Car (the special mission's B-29 bomber) first overflew Kokura as a primary target but diverted to Nagasaki due to visibility concerns. It is theoretically possible that Kokura was indeed the (also pre-demolished) primary target, even for the fake scenario, but I doubt it. It appears that the Urakami Valley was pre-selected for its ideal state of ruin, well in advance of the mission. First, note the idealized targeting rationale in the mission account below, which is at variance with other narratives of the 'lucky cloud break' allowing last-minute access only to a target distant from the (supposedly) pre-planned aiming point.

> Almost the entire population of 230,000 was engaged in the manufacture of arms, munitions, and other war products. Two great Mitsubishi factories were located in the heart of the city. To the north, one of the world's largest torpedo plants. And further south, the huge steel and arms works. The bomb, which was dropped on Nagasaki was aimed at a point midway between the two plants, to be sure to cause

the greatest possible industrial damage. Unlike Nagasaki, the force of the explosion was largely confined to the industrial valley, which was surrounded by a series of hills, which shielded many other areas of the city.

('The Atom Strikes' 1945)

That account is at least honest in one respect. It highlights the obvious military motivation (which existed well before Fat Man) for the US strategic forces' *pre-demolition* of the Urakami valley, operating entirely independently of, and prior to, any awareness of the nuclear option. The industrial part of the city had been pre-demolished, as we've already seen. Contrast the idealized version above with another rendition, below. It seems the air is slowly being let out of the whole Kabuki production:

1158: Upon arriving at Nagasaki, Bockscar has enough fuel for only one pass over the city, even with an emergency landing at Okinawa. Nagasaki is covered with clouds, but one gap allows a drop several miles from the intended aim point. Bombardier Kermit Beahan releases Fat Man.

1202 (11:02 AM Nagasaki time): Fat Man explodes at an altitude of 1,650 feet with a yield of 22,000 kt over the Mitsubishi Steel and Arms Works near the perimeter of the city.

The failure to drop Fat Man at the precise bomb aim point caused the atomic blast to be confined to the Urakami Valley. As a consequence, a major portion of the city was protected from the explosion. The Fat Man was dropped over the city's industrial valley midway between the Mitsubishi Steel and Arms Works in the south and the Mitsubishi-Urakami Ordnance Works in the north.

(Atomic Heritage Foundation)

So now we suddenly have a "drop several miles from" and a "*failure to drop at*" the bomb aim point. They felt they had to use the Urakami valley, as the pre-demolition there was the best available. At the same time, there may have been frets or disagreements in the high command about whether the existing damage there was really adequate to support the sci-fi *wrath-of-heaven* nuclear myth they were building. So they hedged their bets with variable stories, one of which is the present standard narrative that the mission was not executed to spec and therefore the results weren't quite as impressive as would otherwise be expected. But they needn't have worried, as everyone has thoroughly bought into it.

Conveniently, there are no professional military survey photos of the immediate on-the-day aftermath because:

> *The third plane, piloted by Hopkins, arrived three hours later after circling Nagasaki and photographing the damage with an unofficial camera that a young physicist, Harold Agnew, had snuck on board. This was fortuitous. No one on the plane knew how to operate the official camera because the man assigned the task was kicked off before takeoff because he had hastily grabbed a raft instead of a parachute.*
>
> (Bulletin of the Atomic Scientists)

In any case, however it is said to have come about, Fat Man was supposedly dropped on the Urakami Valley area of Nagasaki. Let's take that conventional storyline as the point of departure.

What really happened at Nagasaki is the key to everything – the key to the future and the fate of humanity. That's because, even if the Hiroshima atomic attack was likely faked (as we've seen), indicating that Little Boy was merely a Kabuki nuke, that still leaves the door open for nuclear weapons of the more sophisticated Fat Man design. People talk about the so-called 'Von Neumann architecture' of digital computers – the fundamental processing model still reflected in today's machines. We could talk similarly about the 'Von Neumann nuke'. The imploded plutonium configuration that Von Neumann made possible is the essential basis for everything that comes after – including the fission triggers for the hydrogen super-beasts of the 1950's and beyond. If Hiroshima alone was

FOOL ME TWICE: JAPAN 1945

faked, but Nagasaki was real, we're still screwed. That scenario leaves us with the historical curiosity of the Hiroshima staging for academics to ponder, but humanity remains under the nuclear sword of Damocles.

So. What really happened? Clearly, the Urakami Valley was destroyed in World War II. Let's not entertain any doubts on that score. The questions are, just as with Hiroshima: *when* and *how*? I'm not going to get into the technical aspects of the supposed mission *per se*. I'll deal mostly with the logic of observed effects. You can't criticize a mission where (despite the conventional narrative of missed rendezvous points, insufficient fuel, and targeting snafu's) Murphy's Law seems to have been suspended in that at least the device itself, when finally dropped, did 'work' (supposedly).

Any number of little gotcha's could have prevented it from working to spec. For example, what's to guarantee Fat Man wouldn't freeze at altitude? The first H-bomb feasibility demonstration, coded for the test as Ivy Mike, was triggered by a fission bomb, not dissimilar in basic principle to Fat Man (but sporting some new 'chrome and fins' for sure).

> *The primary stage was a TX-5 boosted fission bomb in a separate space atop the assembly (so it would not **freeze**, rendering it **inoperable**).*
>
> (Wikipedia)

Freeze… inoperable. Fortunately the Fat Man was more robust than its descendant, because even though the B-29's cockpit could be heated, the bomb bay was not. It gets cold at 30,000 feet altitude. But I'm not going to dwell on this kind of trivia. Maybe only the added 'booster' component would be vulnerable to "freezing". All's well that ends well. Let's talk about targeting and ground effects.

Conventional thinking, which of course accepts the Fat Man atomic account, concluded that there was no firestorm in Nagasaki:

> *Although many fires likewise burnt following the bombing, in contrast to Hiroshima where sufficient fuel density was available, no firestorm developed in Nagasaki as the damaged areas did not furnish enough fuel to generate the phenomenon. Instead, the ambient wind at the time pushed the fire spread along the valley.*
>
> (Wikipedia, citing Glasstone, Samuel; Dolan, Philip J., eds. (1977). The Effects of Nuclear Weapons. Washington, D.C.: United States Department of Defense and the Energy Research and Development Administration)

Let's call this the 'Effects' account of the attack, *denying there was any firestorm*. Can that be accurate? No, it's wrong. Even if the obvious on-site evidence doesn't register, in my view it's undeniable that a fire-storm destroyed the Urakami Valley. This is confirmed by the classic photograph of the pyrocumulus cloud rising over Nagasaki, Japan, supposedly 20 minutes after detonation, 9 August 1945, photographed from Koyagi-jima, a small island southwest of Nagasaki.

Fool Me Twice: Japan 1945

Pyrocumulus cloud rising over Nagasaki, Japan, approximately 20 minutes after detonation, 9 August 1945, photographed from Koyagi-jima, a small island southwest of Nagasaki. (Hiromichi Matsuda)

A pyrocumulus cloud is the unmistakable signature of a firestorm. These are observed in firestorms which arise from natural causes such as forest fires and volcanoes.

Death Object

Pyrocumulus cloud rising from a wildfire.

The pyrocumulus cloud is the signature of a firestorm. This was borne out in Hiroshima, was also destroyed by a firestorm.

Hiroshima's firestorm (left) with its signature pyrocumulus cloud (not the atomic mushroom cloud as often wrongly tagged). Twenty minutes after detonation, during the formation of this firestorm, soot-filled black rain began to fall on survivors. A natural firestorm's pyrocumulus (right).

Wildfire pyrocumulus cloud.

Furthermore, the effects on the ground are consistent with that phenomenon. So obviously the 'Effects' account, which denies that the firestorm was possible or took place, is wrong. In fact, many orthodox analysts (i.e. not nutso conspiracy theorists) do accept that a firestorm took place. But strangely enough, those orthodox analysts - who assert that a firestorm did result from Fat Man in the Urakami Valley - are, by their own logic of the bomb, *wrong*. By the accepted logic of the bomb and the hit zone, there in fact should *not* have been a firestorm. The 'Effects' account would actually be correct – by the conventional story.

Have I lost you? Let's ponder in finer detail. If a bomb with the standard cited features of Fat Man had hit a virgin, un-demolished Urakami Valley, there should have been no firestorm. The 'Effects' authors are right that, if it had been a real atomic bomb, *'the damaged areas did not furnish enough fuel to generate the phenomenon'*. Basically there wouldn't have been enough stuff left standing, in any kind of shape to burn, in the narrow confined valley, attacked by a 20 kiloton nuke. It would all have been carbonized, vaporized, blown to dust in an instant. The valley would have been eviscerated. A firestorm needs a standing city as its initial breeding ground. The authors of the 'Effects' report were scripting according to the bomb characteristics, not according to what actually went down that day, and prior to that day, in the Urakami Valley. Obviously the legitimate Nagasaki firestorm photo need not have been shot on the day of the supposed nuke attack. It was probably shot at least a month or two prior.

To summarize: conventional analysts can have their Nagasaki A-bomb – but then they don't get their firestorm. And without the firestorm, it's hard to account for the pyrocumulus cloud photo (and the nature of the destruction in the Valley). On the other hand, they can have their firestorm – but then they can't keep their A-bomb, by the logic cited in the 'Effects' passage. QED.

Downfall

The background you need to understand why Japan surrendered to the bomb and colluded in the scam lies in recognizing that the war was designed more as psy-op than as military practicality from the very beginning.

> *The center of gravity of the problem was missed by the Combined Chiefs of Staff. Had they seen that it lay in interdicting movement and not in fire-raising, surely they would have done what the twelve civilian members of the [United States Strategic Bombing Survey (Pacific War)] suggested should have been done, which was as follows: "A successful attack on the Hakodate rail ferry, the Kanmon tunnels and nineteen bridges and vulnerable sections of line so selected as to set up five separate zones of complete interdiction would have virtually eliminated further coal movements, would have immobilized the remainder of the rail system through lack of coal, and would have completed the strangulation of Japan's economy. This strangulation would have more effectively and efficiently destroyed the economic structure of the country than individually destroying Japan's cities and factories. It would have reduced Japan to a series of isolated communities,*

incapable of any sustained industrial production, incapable of moving food fro the agricultural areas to the cities, and incapable of rapid large-scale movements of troops and munitions. "The Survey believes that such an attack, had it been well-planned in advance, might have been initiated by carrier-based attacks on shipping and on the Hakodate ferry in August, 1944, could have been continued by serial mining of inland waterways beginning in December, 1944, and could have been further continued by initiating the railroad attack as early as April, 1945. The Survey has estimated that force requirements to effect complete interdiction of the railroad system would have been 650 B-29 visual sorties carrying 5,200 tone of high-explosive bombs. Deduct from these figures the 15,000 sorties and 100,000 tones of incendiary bombs dropped on the sixty-six Japanese cities, and the residue is a fair measure of the waste of military means and effort, also of the strategic error (sic!) of the Combined Chiefs of Staff."

('The Second World War, 1939-45: A Strategical And Tactical History' J. F. C. Fuller)

So, vicious as the city bombing campaign undeniably was, it was more for demoralization and punishment than for practical military neutralization. The psy-op aspect of the war persisted into the final nuclear phase as well, with both sides having very strong reasons to buy heavily into the fakeout. Japan had lost the game long before, but as we say: 騎虎の勢い (*it's hard to dismount a tiger*). Given the situation, the atomic story was an absolute godsend.

Though in the United States the story is bomb-centric, in fact the Supreme Council (wartime leadership) did not rush to meet immediately following the news of the Hiroshima bombing. A crisis-mode full meeting *was* convened on August 9th – but that was several days after Hiroshima. Thus Hiroshima did not seem to light a fire under anybody. After all, they'd had 67 cities trashed already and nobody had been pushed to talk seriously about surrender. And neither was Nagasaki the catalyst for this extraordinary gathering. The Supreme Council meeting had been convened that morning *before* Nagasaki was hit.

> At 11:30 A.M., while the Big Six [leaders] were engaged in a heated debate on what to do about the Potsdam terms, news of the second atomic bomb on Nagasaki was relayed to the Supreme War Council. The Nagasaki bomb, however, had little impact on the substance of the discussion. The official history of the Imperial General Headquarters notes: "There is no record in other materials that treated the effect [of the Nagasaki bomb] seriously." Describing the Big Six meeting on this crucial day, neither Togo nor Toyoda mentioned anything about the atomic bomb on Nagasaki.
>
> ('Racing the Enemy: Stalin, Truman, and the Surrender of Japan' Tsuyoshi Hasegawa)

Therefore, *neither* atomic bombing was the event that really spooked the leadership into considering surrender. So what was the urgency? It was this:

> At 11pm Trans-Baikal time on August 8, 1945, Soviet foreign minister Molotov informed Japanese ambassador Satō that the Soviet Union had declared war on the Empire of Japan, and that from August 9 the Soviet Government would consider itself to be at war with Japan.[11] At one minute past midnight Trans-Baikal time on August 9, 1945, the Soviets commenced their invasion simultaneously on three fronts to the east, west and north of Manchuria.
>
> (Wikipedia)

Japan's leaders knew they were in no position to fight a two front war. They understood the immediate proximity and strength of the Russian forces. It was obvious to them that Japan would be invaded and end up partitioned at best, or entirely occupied by the Soviets at worst. This would have intolerable consequences on both the practical and ideological levels. Under the Soviets, there would be little chance of retaining the status of the Emperor, or any semblance of traditional life. The wartime leaders would be blamed for prodding the nation forward to absolute ruin and all would be summarily executed – including the entire Imperial Family (remember the Romanov family).

Soviet attack, not the Hiroshima bomb, convinced political leaders to end the war by accepting the Potsdam Declaration.

('Racing the Enemy: Stalin, Truman, and the Surrender of Japan'
Tsuyoshi Hasegawa)

The war was a complete failure. The glorious Empire of the Sun lay in smoking ruins – *'not one stone atop another'*. Meanwhile the leadership had been feeding the people bullshit all along about how there was still hope, and glorious victories still lay ahead. The concept of 'face' (honor, reputation, shame) is big in Japan. It would be humiliating and dangerous to admit openly that it was time to surrender because we, your divinely infallible leaders, seriously screwed things up by ever starting this in the first place.

But a science fiction weapon, that nobody could withstand, that no strategic genius could have possibly predicted, the very wrath of heaven descending from out of nowhere like a thunderbolt – there's an ideal made-in-Hollywood escape hatch and cover story. Attributing the sudden about-face toward surrender to the A-bomb would also generate sympathy for Japan as a victim of demonic forces rather than a cruel imperialist hegemon, and would also curry favor with American vanity (not to mention the USA's post war international PR plans). Accepting and centralizing the bomb's role as the trigger for the end stage served everybody's interests. And so it came to pass.

Nagasaki hypocenter: curb your bloodlust or suffer the wrath of heaven.

The Mike of the Beast

And I beheld another beast coming up out of the earth; and he had horns like a lamb, and he spake as a dragon. And he exerciseth all the power of the first beast before him, and causeth the earth and them which dwell therein to worship the deadly wound of the first beast... And he doeth great wonders, so that he maketh fire come down from heaven on the earth in the sight of men, And deceiveth them that dwell on the earth by the means of those miracles which he had power to do in the sight of the beast; saying to them that dwell on the earth, that they should make an image of the beast.

(Revelation 13:11-15)

H-Bomb

I haven't said anything about hydrogen bombs so far, and I don't have much to say about them now. The thing is that the H-bomb stands or falls according to the status of the original fission nukes. If explosive fission is truly possible, if the FEAR hypothesis turns out to be true, if Hiroshima and Nagasaki really *were* nuked to oblivion, then forget it. There'd be no reason not to dogpile on with an H-bomb at that point. Remember that hydrogen bombs use fission devices as triggers. At that point, I would put my hands up and surrender, raise the white flag. Nukes are real, fine, have it your way. I wouldn't draw an arbitrary line, saying yes to fission-FEAR, but no to fusion-FEAR (although some of the original Manhattan scientists did hold that position at various times, believing the H-bomb could not work).

Some, if not all, of the H-bomb test films look pretty cheesy. It's amazing what can be done by cleverly combining and editing simple clips of clouds and sunrises via standard video techniques like cropping, zooming, re-timing (faster or slower), Ken Burns, key frames, etc. Not to mention dramatic scary musical scoring.

And when they did sometimes have a chance to blow something up for real, so much the better, more feedstock for the special effects editors to work with. For example, consider the first USA hydrogen bomb test.

> *Ivy Mike was the codename given to the first test of a full-scale thermonuclear device, in which part of the explosive yield comes from nuclear fusion. It was detonated on November 1, 1952 by the United States on the island of Elugelab in Enewetak Atoll, in the Pacific Ocean, as part of Operation Ivy. It was the first full test of the Teller–Ulam design, a staged fusion device. Due to its physical size and fusion fuel type (cryogenic liquid deuterium), the Mike device was not suitable for use as a deliverable weapon; it was intended as an extremely conservative proof of concept experiment to validate the concepts used for multi-megaton detonations.*

(Wikipedia)

Anyway, the thing supposedly worked, although it was noted that 77% of its output was actually fission yield from the uranium tamper within the enclosing cylinder of cryogenic deuterium (a form of hydrogen) fusion fuel:

> *The test was carried out on 1 November 1952 at 07:15 local time (19:15 on 31 October, Greenwich Mean Time). It produced a yield of 10.4 megatons of TNT. However, 77% of the final yield came from fast fission of the uranium tamper, which produced large amounts of radioactive fallout.*

(Wikipedia)

It's a good thing all that fission worked so well actually, given that in fusion reactor experimentation:

> *Typical fuel pellets (deuterium + tritium) are about the size of a pinhead and contain around 10 milligrams of fuel: in practice, only a small proportion of this fuel will undergo fusion, but if all this fuel were consumed it would release the energy equivalent to burning a barrel of oil.*
>
> (Wikipedia)

Or, in the case of a bomb, the energy equivalent to exploding a barrel of oil. Therefore, you can picture the hydrogen/fusion part of the bomb as a mountain of oil barrels being torched but only partially ignited. An impressive light show, but of course the fission does the heavy lifting. In fact, the hydrogen bomb is mainly just a way of getting more bang for your fission buck. Fusion produces lots of neutrons so by clever mutual reinforcement of the two processes (fission to trigger fusion, fusion in turn generating more and 'hotter' neutrons for additional fission) you increase overall (putative) yield.

Working from the FAIL hypothesis requires us to take a stagecraft point of view though, because FAIL does not admit the reality of explosive fission chain reactions in the first place. The name "hydrogen bomb" probably does not refer to real fusion of deuterium into helium. It's more likely the name is applied based on the main conventional element used in the show. For the films they probably blew up a huge cylinder of hydrogen (possibly spiked as yet another dirty bomb production). Remember the Hindenburg!

Death Object

The Hindenburg begins to blow.

Lookout Mountain Studios

Whatever happened in the demo, they were able to jack it up with some special effects applied by a secretive quasi-governmental film unit in Los Angeles.

> *The entire [Ivy Mike] shot was documented by the filmmakers of Lookout Mountain studios. A post production explosion sound was overdubbed over what was a completely silent detonation from the vantage point of the camera, with the blast wave sound only arriving a number of seconds later, as akin to thunder, with the exact time depending on its distance. The film was also accompanied by powerful, Wagner-esque music featured on many test films of that period and was hosted by actor Reed Hadley. A private screening was given to*

President Dwight D. Eisenhower in 1953, after he succeeded President Harry S. Truman. In 1954, the film was released to the public after censoring, and was shown on commercial television channels.

(Wikipedia)

As for the Laurel Canyon unit:

What would become known as Lookout Mountain Laboratory was originally envisioned as an air defense center. Built in 1941 and nestled in two-and-a-half secluded acres off what is now Wonderland Park Avenue, the installation was hidden from view and surrounded by an electrified fence. By 1947, the facility featured a fully operational movie studio. In fact, it is claimed that it was perhaps the world's only completely self-contained movie studio. With 100,000 square feet of floor space, the covert studio included sound stages, screening rooms, film processing labs, editing facilities, an animation department, and seventeen climate-controlled film vaults. It also had underground parking, a helicopter pad and a bomb shelter.

Over its lifetime, the studio produced some 19,000 classified motion pictures – more than all the Hollywood studios combined (which I guess makes Laurel Canyon the real 'motion picture capital of the world'). Officially, the facility was run by the U.S. Air Force and did nothing more nefarious than process AEC footage of atomic and nuclear bomb tests. The studio, however, was clearly equipped to do far more than just process film. There are indications that Lookout Mountain Laboratory had an advanced research and development department that was on the cutting edge of new film technologies. Such technological advances as 3-D effects were apparently first developed at the Laurel Canyon site. And Hollywood luminaries like John Ford, Jimmy Stewart, Howard Hawks, Ronald Reagan, Bing Crosby, Walt Disney and Marilyn Monroe were given clearance to work at the facility on undisclosed projects. There is no indication that any of them ever spoke of their work at the clandestine studio.

('Weird Scenes Inside the Canyon' Dave McGowan)

Death Object

Lookout Mountain studio poster.

Something Fishy: Bikini

Let's take another look at Bikini atoll.

> *The nuclear testing at Bikini Atoll program was a series of 23 nuclear devices detonated by the United States between 1946 and 1958 at seven test sites on the reef itself, on the sea, in the air and underwater. The test weapons produced a combined fission yield of 42.2 Mt of explosive power.*
>
> (Wikipedia)

One particularly nasty test was held there.

> *Castle Bravo was the first in a series of high-yield thermonuclear weapon design tests conducted by the United States at Bikini Atoll, Marshall Islands, as part of Operation Castle. Detonated on March 1, 1954, the device was the most powerful nuclear device detonated by the United States, and its first lithium-deuteride-fueled thermonuclear weapon. Castle Bravo's yield was 15 megatons of TNT, 2.5 times more than predicted.*
>
> (Wikipedia)

Here is what the blast map for Bravo would look like over the Bikini atoll:

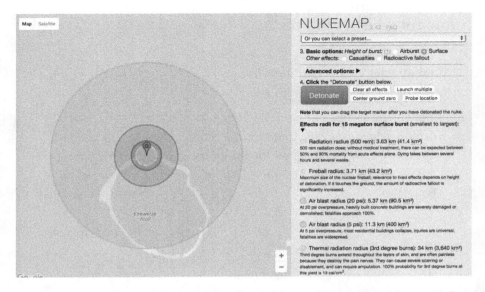

15 megaton Bravo test covered Bikini atoll with blast and heat. (see Bibliography for full credit of map and overlay).

Here we have a few miles of fragile coral reef, elevated only a few feet above sea level, that was subjected to a sustained atomic attack of massed overwhelming heat, blast and radiation power never before known on this planet. The sand and limestone of the ground, beaches, and lagoon floor by rights should have been fused into a disgusting lunar slag, the kind of thing you find on the higher reaches of the austere Kilauea volcano in Hawaii – a total moonscape. But in fact the place looks more like an undeveloped version of Waikiki.

> [At Hiroshima], *solid materials on the ground immediately below the burst probably attained surface temperatures of 3,000 to 4,000°C (5,400 to 7,200°F).*
>
> ('The Effects of Nuclear Weapons' Glasstone and Dolan)
>
> *When first erupted from a volcanic vent, lava is a liquid usually at temperatures from 700 to 1,200 °C (1,292 to 2,192 °F).*
>
> (Wikipedia)

The Mike of the Beast

Keep in mind that virtually every one of these dozens of tests was very far beyond the yield power of Little Boy and Fat Man. Yet as far as I know, nobody traveling from Bikini has reported any *bikinitite* analogous to the *trinitite* discussed earlier. In fact the place seems to be fine, apart from some low level radiation in the crabs. Though Bikini is remote, since there'd be money to make from selling *bikinite*, somebody would already be doing it, because a tourist program has now begun.

> *After the 23 nuclear explosions that the United States conducted on this remote coral atoll in the 1940's and 50's, one almost expects to visit today and find just a few charred islets surrounded by brackish water emitting an eerie glow. So the amazing thing about Bikini is how alive it is: a white sand island full of coconut palms swaying over a perfect turquoise sea, fish and sea turtles swimming languorously by the beach. There are also a few tourists, and many more are expected, because Bikini is now once more open to the public.*
>
> (The New York Times, March 5, 1997)

Bikini atoll's 'Castle Koon' test site - 110 kilotons (almost 6x Fat Man) detonated from a barge just offshore in the lagoon. If you viewed this photograph in color you'd see lush green, sandy beach, clear lagoon, healthy sea vegetation. The average elevation of Bikini atoll is 2 meters above sea level (7 feet).

There are many oddities about the Bikini test history (even the total test count varies, by source, from 23 'explosions' to 67 – it's true that a few were planned but cancelled, not enough to account for all the variation). One interesting feature of the atoll is the concrete cap over the Cactus test crater, on Runit Island. The 'Cactus Dome' is a concrete cover over a test crater that was pressed into service as a dump for a scrape of supposed radioactive topsoil from the atoll's islands. Just barely offshore from this hole is the leftover crater from another test, Redwing-Lacrosse. Here's how the two craters stack up against one another:

Hardtack-Cactus (surface): 18 kilotons, 350 feet diameter crater.
Redwing-Lacrosse (surface): 40 kilotons, 600 feet diameter crater.

The diameter figure for Lacrosse is specified by Wikipedia's 'Redwing' entry data table as follows (as of early 2017, until corrected as a result of this book):

> *Mockup of the TX-39. Left a visible Crater off Runit Island, next to Cactus Dome, 600 ft (180 m) in diameter.*
>
> (Wikipedia 'Operation Redwing'; row 'Lacrosse' in data table)

So far so good, a double blast yield should leave approximately double the damage (crater size) and indeed that's what is usually reported on paper, as you see above. Likewise, in physical reality the Lacrosse crater should be pretty much double the size of the Cactus crater.

But it clearly isn't. They are about the same size. And don't think the Cactus Dome was overfilled beyond the crater, because every source that gives specs for the Dome itself specifies a figure somewhere in the 300 to 350 range, which can be verified by measuring across the satellite photos. It's the same as the reported diameter of the original explosion crater. If you then measure across the map of the Lacrosse crater in various places and take an average, the diameter there comes to about 375 feet diameter. In reality the two craters are basically the same size.

The Mike of the Beast

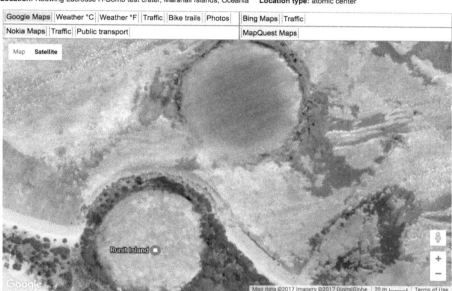

Cactus Dome filled-in test crater (bottom) with adjacent Lacrosse crater. They are essentially the same size.

Why has it been reported so divergently? No good answer. There may be sources that report a more accurate (smaller) diameter for the Lacrosse crater than Wikipedia does. But that will simply beg the question again: why *are* they the same size, when one bomb was twice the yield of the other? Though Lacrosse was on a platform above very shallow water, both are characterized as 'Surface' bursts. Seems like their overall conditions were too similar to allow for an altitude or topographic factor in such a surprising outcome (craters of identical size).

It would be lunatic to fantasize that the Lacrosse 'crater' *of the same size* was made simply by dredging fake fill from the lagoon floor for the immediately adjacent Cactus. Nobody in his right mind would hint for even a moment that they buried a lot of soil, not because it *is* radioactive, but precisely because it *isn't* (and leaving that lying around openly wouldn't be good for the story).

But I should chill out and cut slack. It's not like tens of millions of dollars were spent on preparing, conducting, and analyzing these tests. It's not 'real science' or anything, so I should ease up and leave some wiggle room. I adduce this one example merely to illustrate the interesting oddities that crop up all over the Bikini history when you begin to 'dig' into it.

Cloudy Skies

There are many interesting anomalies in the Bikini aerial footage also. Sometimes the same explosion begins in an atmosphere with a thick low cloud ceiling in one photo sequence, while another sequence of the same test shows clear, bright and sunny skies. That may be just a POV problem.

One of the most beautiful tests was the Crossroads Baker underwater blast which we examined earlier in the context of comparative crater sizes. The Crossroads tests were pre-gamed at miniature scale, well in advance, under very realistic simulated conditions.

Pre-game modeling work for Crossroads.

SCALE MODEL "ATOMIC BOMB" TESTS. In preparation for the Bikini tests a number of scale model experiments were conducted at the Taylor Model Basin near Washington D. C. to aid in estimating the size and character of waves that would be produced by the actual atomic bomb explosions. Scale model Victory ships were constructed of thin sheets of brass and floated in the "lagoon" shown above. Scaled amounts of TNT were used to simulate the atomic bombs. These tests were made in a specially-constructed tank known as "Little Bikini." Other studies were made on a larger scale, using 500-pound amounts of explosive, in tests conducted at the Naval Mine Warfare Test Station at Patuxent, Maryland. In both types of scaled experiments effects noted were the size of the water crater, height, persistency and diffusion of plumes.

('Operation Crossroads The Official Pictorial Record')

Death Object

The Taylor Model Basin (referred to in the photo description) is a giant indoor ship testing facility that functions as a perfect sound stage for simulating any kind of naval operation.

It's interesting to examine the effect of Baker's huge nuclear shock wave on puffy little clouds which obstruct its path. The photo planes (manned and drones) for the Baker shot were circling at about 10,000 feet altitude. In the sequence of film frames, we note a small cloud at the start. It is between the photo plane and the burst. This is a cumulus cloud.

Cumulus clouds are often described as "puffy", "cotton-like" or "fluffy" in appearance, and being low-level clouds, are generally less than 2,000 m (6,600 ft) in altitude.
(Wikipedia)

This cloud is subsequently engulfed by the plume and also hit by the shockwave.

The Mike of the Beast

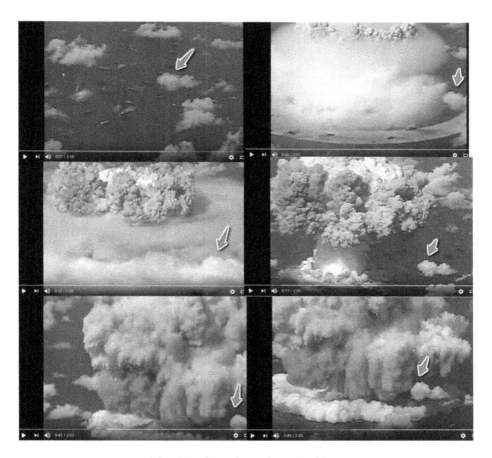

Cloud tracking through a nuke blast.

In the photo sequence, we see at top left the pre-detonation scene, time 00:01. A puffy little cumulus rests below and beneath the photo plane, between it and the blast. At time 00:06, the camera shifts left to center the detonation, cloud unchanged as neither blast wave nor plume have arrived yet. Between 00:11 and 00:13 things get weird, because our little cloud is completely enveloped in the plume/vapor of the blast. Though it looks kind of 'roided up, our cloud is hiding at (or inside) the indicated location. The blast wave also rocked the plane and camera at about this point, 00:10 to 00:11. That's acceptable 'effecting' if we take the blast wave propagation at somewhere in the neighborhood of the speed of sound. Well before 00:17 (shown in following panel), the cloud has resumed its exact original shape and position. The lower left panel 00:41 results from an unexplained extreme M-shaped up and down jolting of the camera and/or plane. By 00:49 at the bottom right, everything's centered back to normal.

When the air is locally disturbed by the nuclear blast shock wave, a condensation/vapor cloud should disappear or at least be distorted and/or moved. Note that the mild 'bending' effect seen in rocket trails commonly fired at nuclear tests is (by hypothesis) something entirely different, That is an optical effect in the intervening atmosphere, not a direct impact of the blast onto the vapor trail. But here we don't even get any bending, hooking or breaking as sometimes noted in the rocket trails.

Photo and Film Checklist

The New York Times claimed in a 2010 article that "*in all, the atomic moviemakers fashioned 6,500 secret films, all over the world*". It's impossible to go through every film to micro-analyze all the anomalies frame-by-frame. But certain strange features occur often enough to form a preliminary checklist for critical analysis. I'm not claiming that the presence of any or all of these issues in any one given film totally invalidates the FEAR hypothesis. The FEAR hypothesis is already laid down and out for the count before the bell even rang for this chapter. I don't rely on second-guessing movie special effects. Nevertheless, as you do your own research it may be interesting to note how often these little gotcha's crop up.

<u>Sound effects</u>: Most of the test films are cheesed up with the goofy Wagnerian Muzak-like noise (mentioned above), to excite and inspire us with the glory of it all. Very offensive but what can you do? Such was the state of human evolution when these were made and probably now too. More to the point though, for those clips *without* the Nukezak, trying to give off more of an 'authentic' vibe, watch out for craftily *misaligned initial blast sound*. Knowing the education level of the average fool at whom these masterpieces were aimed, the filmmakers have almost always shfited the blast sound back (to time it with the initial flash). As far as is known, only one or two films that purport to incorporate authentic blast sound have done so with 'Original Timing!©' (still fake of course, by the

FAIL hypothesis). Not a 'smoking gun', because it's a known 'thing' even in the conventional analysis community, but just something to watch for. It shows that they are perfectly willing to game the tape for emotional effect (and to meet the Dumbo audience's expectations).

Shadows: It's common in nuke test photos and films to observe no significant change in sunlight shadows caused by the blast. Often there's only contrast or exposure change (if any change at all) – things that are easily manipulated in the darkroom.

Shadows tend to be oddly unaffected by the atomic light at instant of the blast said to be 'brighter than a thousand suns'.

Crazy cuts: The films cut all over the place, back and forth between long shots, close-ups, audience reaction, effect on materials, and so on. It doesn't prove anything underhanded, but tends to distract from careful sequential observation.

Static Segments: Sometimes portions of an otherwise fast-evolving blast cloud or effect scene are static, while a single privileged or highlighted element develops along the time track. The reverse is also sometimes seen (everything *except* a static central element continues to evolve)

<u>Mystery POV</u>: Sometimes it's hard to imagine how a given shot was obtained short of a studio sound-stage close-up.

Conspiracy!

> *It is one of those instances where the reasoner can produce an effect which seems remarkable to his neighbour, because the latter has missed the one little point which is the basis of the deduction.*
>
> (Sherlock Holmes)

We've gone through some intense material up to this point. Let's take a philosophy break now. There seems to be a culture clash between so-called 'conspiracy theorists' on one side of the divide and defenders of rational orthodoxy on the other. Conspiracy theorists propose and defend unconventional interpretations of events and motives. Such analyses (including this book) are viewed by defenders of orthodox thought as absolute drooling idiocy.

Let's call those who regard themselves as rational, sober, mature, informed, emotionally stable defenders of common sense and scientific fidelity the soldiers of '*Consensus Reality Ontologically Certain Knowing*' (CROCK) - upholders of truth. They are camels never straying from the desert of the real. I don't mean to poke fun at either side. I totally get each side's point of view. Conspiracy people really are a little too whacked out some of the time. And the CROCK people are too anally uptight for my taste. Con artists always say that those who are most certain they cannot be fooled make the best marks. And at bottom both populations are just people, struggling for survival, satisfaction, and significance in this cold world.

Apart from the validity of any one theory (conventional or conspiratorial), it's interesting to look at the *psychology* of both sides. The masters of CROCK love nothing better than armchair psychoanalysis of conspiracy theorists. When they ask themselves why anybody would believe the patently lunatic bullshit which the average conspiracy guy takes as revealed truth, they always come up with some version of the following list:

- Ignorance (of science)
- Compensation (wanting to feel special)
- Anxiety (seeking certainty to alleviate fear)
- Boredom (helping to enliven an otherwise lackluster day)
- Avarice (selling books, lecture seats)
- Perversity (trolls, haters, teenagers)

Let's go through these one at a time.

Ignorance: The CROCKsters have a point here. Your typical conspiracy theorist is not as well versed in techie subjects as he or she ought to be. Yet they often opine on highly technical areas that lie outside their core competence. (if they even *have* a core competence).

Compensation: The conspiracy theorist is taken to be a basement-dwelling loser/loner who buttresses himself in the face of the world's indifference or rejection with the false solace of knowing more than his betters. It's ego reinforcement. Of course there's a certain half-life to that. As time passes and the content of any given conspiracy theory becomes more widely known, the cachet of holding 'secret' knowledge about what's really happening tends to diminish.

Anxiety: It's assumed that the conspiracy theorist can't handle the harshness of the real world, thus they escape to a fantasy world. A world they can understand, control, interpret to others and generally own.

Boredom: Speaks for itself. Reality can be (perceived as) boring, but with unlimited mental fantasy yarn you can weave any exciting story, of infinite threat or promise.

Avarice: The average conspiracy theorist just poking around the web may not make much, but people who run the larger conspiracy blogs and sites probably make *hundreds*, maybe even *thousands* of dollars a year from their stuff! Possibly more. With *that* kind of money in the game, bad actors will always be tempted to try their hand.

Perversity: A non-trivial percentage of conspiracy types are just trouble-making trolls, not even sincere in their wickedness, just spoiling for the attention that a keyboard flame war radiates. These people will say anything for a laugh and to get a rise out of the comically serious and amusingly provoke-able camels of CROCK.

Very satisfying! The trouble is that the above analysis of conspiracy nuts has bilateral symmetry. It's sauce for both goose and gander. It can easily be turned around and replayed from the other side without loss of generality. Let's try that.

Ignorance: Here in this one area, the CROCKsters do have valid point. More science is always good. That's why we need some open proof of the nuclear FEAR hypothesis.

Compensation: Emotional compensation is another double-edged putdown. Isn't there a lot of emotional satisfaction in feeling that you are a good citizen, a sober soldier of rationality? You command the high ground of logic and proof, you have education, authority and rationality - all on your side. Isn't that a warm feeling for the orthodox rationalist?

Anxiety: I sometimes wonder why it's supposed to be much more reassuring to suspect that your government or other trusted authorities are out to scam and kill you or other innocents, rather than reposing in the safe certainty that you are in the soft hands of a responsible, adult, protective authority (CROCK). When CROCK psychologizes and tsk-tsk's about conspiracy theorists, you're bound at some point to see a line like this: '*People love certainty and find uncertainty uncomfortable*'. But who is more certain of him or her self than a soldier of CROCK? They know that the USA military would *never* conduct bioweapons experiments on uninformed enlisted men, nor would the CIA have had programs to influence the media, newspapers, academia, etc. Conspiracy theories are treated like the field of AI, as an infinitely receding horizon. As soon as a conspiracy theory turns out to be true, it's pulled over the velvet rope of respectability and is no longer credited to the lunatics' scorecard.

Boredom: I have heard it said, by Richard Dawkins and other defenders of the status quo that reality is much more exciting and beautiful when you look it squarely and honestly in the eye. So I have to assume that CROCKsters are seeking excitement and entertainment by their cleaving to the orthodox, deriving much the same psychological benefit that conspiracy nuts are said to receive from their fantasies.

Avarice: Whoa, champ! Do you *really* want to throw down on *this* particular point? I wonder whether the combined total income from books, websites, speaking engagements or other activities of every major conspiracy theorist in the world exceeds the weekly take from a single soda vending machine in one staff lounge at the Lawrence Livermore weapons lab. It certainly doesn't amount to trillions of dollars, decade after decade.

Perversity: Here I'll grant that a true soldier of CROCK is not normally a mischievous Internet troll. They have a rigid and passionate sincerity. Credit where due.

The point is that these sides are largely mirror images of one another, satisfying the same needs in opposite ways. The soldiers of CROCK rationality are mostly *projecting their own qualities* (anxiety, ego, greed, etc.) onto their mouth-breathing, knuckle-dragging opposite numbers in the conspiracy camp. That doesn't mean one side isn't wrong though. CROCK is probably mostly correct. But isn't there *some* value in having a few outliers, like mutant rogue genes that may cause trouble but could be an ace in the hole when a monolithic genome is attacked?

Strange bedfellows pop up in the eternal cat and mouse game of CROCK vs conspiracy. For example, a few years back, a chemical and/or fuel dump blew up in Tianjin, China.

> *On 12 August 2015, a series of explosions killed 173 people and injured hundreds of others at a container storage station at the Port of Tianjin. The first two explosions occurred within 30 seconds of each other*

at the facility, which is located in the Binhai New Area of Tianjin, China. The second explosion was far larger and involved the detonation of about 800 tonnes of ammonium nitrate. Fires caused by the initial explosions continued to burn uncontrolled throughout the weekend, repeatedly causing secondary explosions, with eight additional explosions occurring on 15 August. The cause of the explosions was not immediately known, but an investigation concluded in February 2016 that an overheated container of dry nitrocellulose was the cause of the initial explosion.

(Wikipedia)

So far so good. But at some point a bunch of conspiracy theorists got all worked up about how this must have been a *nuclear explosion*. So they trotted out all kinds of crazy numbers about possible yield and temperature and blast effects etc. Now, say what you will about me, call me a whacko nutjob, but at least you'll never catch me in *that* particular conspiracy camp. Obviously! Anyway, the defenders of CROCK naturally had to rise to this stupid bait and laboriously *debunk* the nuke suspicions. Which they did very competently I must say. Hats off. For example, the nuke people were saying: *Look at the huge crater! Only a nuke could or would blast out that size of hole!* And they trotted out a photo apparently showing a gigantic nasty pit.

Tianjin, China: huge nuclear crater?

But the defenders of the real would have none of it, trumping and silencing the opposition by pointing out that this 'crater' was more a man-made lake of sorts, created by natural drainage and filling of a shallow blast depression. The dry version isn't nearly as scary-looking.

Tianjin 'blast' crater now dry - minus the firefighter's drainage water.

Going farther afield now, imagine the USA mil.gov had indeed created real nukes but, for whatever tactical reason, was intent on keeping them absolutely *secret*, and was committed to denial, *even when they were used*? In this alternative world, the mil.gov would have announced that Hiroshima was merely a firebombing, etc. Then, ironically, you'd have 'conspiracy theorists' insisting on the *existence* of nuclear weapons (which in this fantasy scenario, would be *true*) while the defenders of CROCK, who always toe to the line drawn by authority, would be strenuously debunking, saying how ridiculous it is to talk about crazy science fiction weapons that blow up cities with a few kilograms worth of 'binding energy' and proving that the destruction was due to ordinary incendiary raids and so on. Thus do the authorities play us like hand puppets. But I don't resent them for it. That is their job.

How many times have I said that *trickery is the way of war*? Is that really such a radical and controversial notion? This has been known since the Trojan Horse. The great Chinese general Zhu Geliang (181–234 CE) was celebrated for baffling the enemy with his infinite tricks and scams. The world has been at continuous war since the middle of the last century with no end in sight. Though I deplore the inhumanity and waste of it all, deep down I'd frankly be a little disappointed if the leaders and 'powers that be' were *not* creative and energetic enough to come up with some really good scams from time to time, like this nuclear thing. But now maybe enough is enough.

Fire No Time: Falsification

Father, Father, we don't need to escalate.
War is not the answer,
For only love can conquer hate.

Marvin Gaye

Skeptics (wait, who *is* the real 'skeptic' here anyway?) may retort that this book has presented only circumstantial evidence - no direct proof. And conspiracy theorists are usually derided for seizing obsessively on small, natural anomalies and making a big effing deal of them. Doh! *How could it be otherwise?* All the direct proof one way or the other is totally classified. A good detective *necessarily works from small clues*. Anyway, in science it is said that hypotheses (apart from formal math and logic) cannot be *proven* – they can only be *falsified*. We've gotten off to a good start on that job with this book. The job of proof falls to those who assert the existence of the superweapons.

Perhaps you're rolling your eyes now, like: *DUDE! There's been megatons of incontrovertible evidence!* By that you mean the reports and films of tests, witness testimonies, historical accounts, etc. I get that. But the ultimate falsification would be a city well and truly nuked to green glass parking lot oblivion. It could be yours. So you better hope my FAIL theory is never finally falsified. You better pray that The Bomb is nothing but a flash-bang device for show.

There's a great story in Richard Rhodes' classic history of the H-bomb where he tells of a tense moment in the run-up to developing 'Joe 1', the first Soviet nuclear weapon.

> On one occasion, writes Zukerman, "they were readying an experiment involving a large explosive charge, over one hundred kilograms. Suddenly the charge caught fire. In such cases, the burn can trigger a detonation, with all its consequences. [The group leader] stayed calm and collected. He led his brigade to the bunker and phoned the dispatcher to order everyone to keep away from the area. This time, nature was kind: there was never an explosion and the charge burned down without incident." Accidents were acts of sabotage in [Beria's Soviet security regime]. The scientists attributed the fire to spontaneous combustion – a passing bird had shat on the charge, they claimed, and the splash of liquid had functioned as a lens to focus the sunlight. It was a story only technological illiterates would swallow, and the bosses did.
>
> ('Dark Sun' Richard Rhodes)

Don't be those guys. If this book's FAIL hypothesis is true, that knowledge is guarded way more deeply and fearfully than the compressibility factors for all six (or seven!) allotropes of plutonium. That would be totally *'Shoot On Sight Eyes Only'* stuff. If, on the other hand, the FEAR hypothesis is correct, the human race is well and truly screwed. Stick a fork in us. We're done.

THE END

Acknowledgements

Special thanks and deepest gratitude to the following friends and colleagues who have reviewed and critiqued portions of this work. All opinions, conclusions, and any errors of fact or interpretation are strictly the author's. Wherever, in some cases, I have morphed your name(s) at your request, well, you know who you are and how valuable your input has been.

Thomas Godfrey, Don Sunada, Peter Hughes, Umeko Chiba, Uday Dhawan, Frank Quinn, Nancy D'Auria, Felix Lake, Shirong Xie, Zimin Qiu, Nini Doi, Frank Leavey, Samuel Danenberg, Fumihiro Suzuki, Eric Su, Jin Nagasawa, Umeji Bando, Indira Ranganathan.

Bibliography

(1) SPECIAL ATTRIBUTION:
Illustration of 'Little Boy' uranium bomb internals:

Based on an illustration by FastFission (Image: Gun-type Nuclear weapon.png) and a modified version by Howard Morland (Image: Gun-Type Fission Weapon .png). The bullet and the target were slightly modified (the bullet was a stack of rings per John Coster-Mullen research: *Atom Bombs The Top Secret Story of Little Boy and Fat Man*')

Author Vector version by Dake with English labels by Papa Lima Whiskey, lines modified by Mfield. As posted: en.wikipedia.org/wiki/Little_Boy

(2) SPECIAL ATTRIBUTION:
All 'blast maps' showing blast contour ring overlaid onto real locations:

nuclearsecrecy.com/nukemap/ is a very useful and educational website that allows the user to see extent of effects (thermal, radiation, and other) damage with any yield, at any detonation height, centered on any GoogleMaps location.

Created by Alex Wellerstein, 2012-2017. NUKEMAP is sponsored by:
The College of Arts and Letters, Stevens Institute of Technology. I assume that Professor Wellerstein generously allows public domain use of derived works from the site, paying it forward as his own site relies on Google's (Alphabet Corp.) generous permission to create his own derived works based on GoogleMaps.

(3) REFERENCES

Baggott, J. E. *The First War of Physics: The Secret History of the Atom Bomb, 1939-1949*. New York: Pegasus, 2011.

Bernstein, Jeremy. *Plutonium a History of the World's Most Dangerous Element*. Sydney, N.S.W.: New South, 2009.

Bird, Kai, and Martin J. Sherwin. *American Prometheus: The Triumph and Tragedy of J. Robert Oppenheimer*. London: Atlantic, 2009.

Bradley, F. J. *No Strategic Targets Left*. Paducah, KY: Turner Pub. 1999.

Burke-Gaffney, Brian. *The Light of Morning Memoirs of the Nagasaki Atomic Bomb Survivors*. Nagasaki-shi, Japan: Nagasaki National Peace Memorial Hall for the Atomic Bomb Victims, 2005.

Cimino, Al. *The Manhattan Project: The Making of the Atomic Bomb*. London: Arcturus, 2016.

Corley, Edwin. *The Jesus Factor*. New York: Stein and Day, 1984.

Coster-Mullen, John. *Atom Bombs: The Top Secret inside Story of the Little Boy and Fat Man*. Waukesha, WI: 2002.

De Seversky Alexander. *Air Power, Key to Survival*. New York: Simon & Schuster, 1950.

Ford, Kenneth. *Building the H Bomb: A Personal History*. London: World Scientific, 2015.

Frank, Richard B. *Downfall: The End of the Imperial Japanese Empire*. New York: Penguin, 2001.

Fuller, J. F. C. *The Second World War, 1939-45: A Strategical And Tactical History*. Da Capo Press, 1993.

Ganguli, Kisari Mohan., and Pratpacandra Rya. *The Mahabharata of Krishna-Dwaipayana Vyasa*. New Delhi: Munshiram Manoharlal, 2001.

Glasstone, Samuel and Philip J. Dolan, *The Effects of Nuclear Weapons*, Third Edition, United States Department of Defense and the United States Department of Energy, 1977.

Groueff, Stephane. *Manhattan Project*. Boston: Little, Brown, 1967.

Groves, Leslie R. *Now It Can Be Told*. Harper & Brothers, 1963.

Gusterson, Hugh. *People of the Bomb: Portraits of America's Nuclear Complex*. Minneapolis, MN: U of Minnesota, 2004.

Harris, Michael. *Atomic Times: My H-bomb Year at the Pacific Proving Ground*. Presidio, 2006.

Hasegawa, Tsuyoshi. *Racing the Enemy: Stalin, Truman, and the Surrender of Japan*. Cambridge, MA: Belknap of Harvard UP, 2006.

Herken, Gregg. *Brotherhood of the Bomb: The Tangled Lives and Loyalties of Robert Oppenheimer, Ernest Lawrence, and Edward Teller*. New York: Henry Holt, 2003.

Hersey, John. *Hiroshima: John Hersey*. New York: Spark Pub., 2002.

Hiltzik, Michael. *Big Science: Ernest Lawrence and the Invention That Launched the Military-industrial Complex*. New York: Simon & Schuster, 2016.

Hines, Neal O. *Proving Ground; an Account of the Radiobiological Studies in the Pacific, 1946-1961*. Seattle: U of Washington, 1962.

Hoddeson, Lillian. *Critical Assembly: A Technical History of Los Alamos during the Oppenheimer Years, 1943-1945*. Cambridge: Cambridge U, 2004.

Hoyt, Edwin P. *Inferno: The Firebombing of Japan, March 9-August 15, 1945*. Lanham, MD: Madison, 2000.

Hull, Mcallister. *Rider of the Pale Horse: A Memoir of Los Alamos and beyond*. Place of Publication Not Identified: Univ Of New Mexico, 2015.

Johnston, Barbara Rose., and Holly M. Barker. *The Consequential Damages of Nuclear War*. N.p.: Left Coast, 2008.

Kelly, Cynthia C., ed. *The Manhattan Project the Birth of the Atomic Bomb in the Words of Its Creators, Eyewitnesses, and Historians.* New York: Tess Press, 2007.

Krauth, Werner. *Statistical Mechanics: Algorithms and Computations.* Oxford: Oxford UP, 2015.

Kunetka, James W. *The General and the Genius: Groves and Oppenheimer: the Unlikely Partnership That Built the Atom Bomb.* Washington: Regnery Publ., 2015.

Kuran, Peter. *How to Photograph an Atomic Bomb.* Santa Clarita, Ca.: VCE, 2006.

Laurence, William L. *Story of the Atomic Bomb.* Wildside, 2009.

McGowan, David. *Weird Scenes inside the Canyon: Laurel Canyon, Covert Ops & the Dark Heart of the Hippie Dream.* London: Headpress, 2014.

Morland, Howard. *The Secret That Exploded.* New York: Random House, 1981.

McPhee, John A. *The Curve of Binding Energy.* New York: Farrar, Straus and Giroux, 1973.

Nahin, Paul J. *Chases and Escapes: The Mathematics of Pursuit and Evasion.* Princeton, N.J: Princeton UP, 2012.

Newman, M. E. J. *Computational Physics.* Createspace, 2013.

Oppenheimer, J. Robert, Charles Weiner, and Alice Kimball Smith. *Robert Oppenheimer: Letters and Recollections.* Cambridge, MA: Harvard UP, 1980.

Osada, Arata. *Children of the A-bomb: The Testament of the Boys and Girls of Hiroshima.* New York: G. P. Putnam's Sons, 1963.

Pellegrino, Charles R. *To Hell and Back: The Last Train from Hiroshima.* Rowman & Littlefield Publishers, 2015.

Rhodes, Richard. *Dark Sun: The Making of the Hydrogen Bomb.* New York: Simon & Schuster Paperbacks, 2005.

Rhodes, Richard. *The Making of the Atom Bomb*. London: Penguin, 1988.

Serber, Robert, and Richard Rhodes. *The Los Alamos Primer: The First Lectrues on How to Build an Atomic Bomb*. Berkeley: U of California, 1992.

Sanger, S. L., and Craig Wollner. *Working on the Bomb: An Oral History of WWII Hanford*. Portland, OR: Portland State U, Continuing Education, 1995.

Schlosser, Eric. *Command and Control: Nuclear Weapons, the Damascus Accident, and the Illusion of Safety*. New York: Penguin, 2014.

Sethna, James P. *Statistical Mechanics: Entropy, Order Parameters, and Complexity*. Oxford: Oxford UP, 2012.

Sherwin, Martin J. *A World Destroyed: Hiroshima and Its Legacies*. Stanford, CA: Stanford UP, 2003.

Siracusa, Joseph M. *Nuclear Weapons: A Very Short Introduction*. Oxford: Oxford U, 2008.

Smyth, Henry De Wolf. *Atomic Energy for Military Purposes*. Lancaster, Penn.: Published for the American Physical Society by the American Institute of Physics, 1945.

Swinson, Marilyn. *Scars of War*. Bloomington IN: IUniverse, 2011.

The Atomic Bombings of Hiroshima and Nagasaki. United States: Manhattan Engineer District, 1945.

Tibbets, Paul W. *The Tibbets Story*. Stein and Day, 1978.

Trumbull, R. *Nine Who Survived Hiroshima and Nagasaki*. New York: Dutton, 1958.

* * *

About the Author

Akio Nakatani is a Professor of Applied Mathematics and Statistics. His research interests include Stochastic Systems, Parameter Estimation, Stochastic Optimization, Monte Carlo Methods and Simulation, Neural Networks, Statistical Pattern Recognition, Statistical Image Analysis, Nonparametric Bayes and Bayesian Hierarchical Models, Time Series, Graphical Models, Nonparametric Bayes and Bayesian Hierarchical Models.